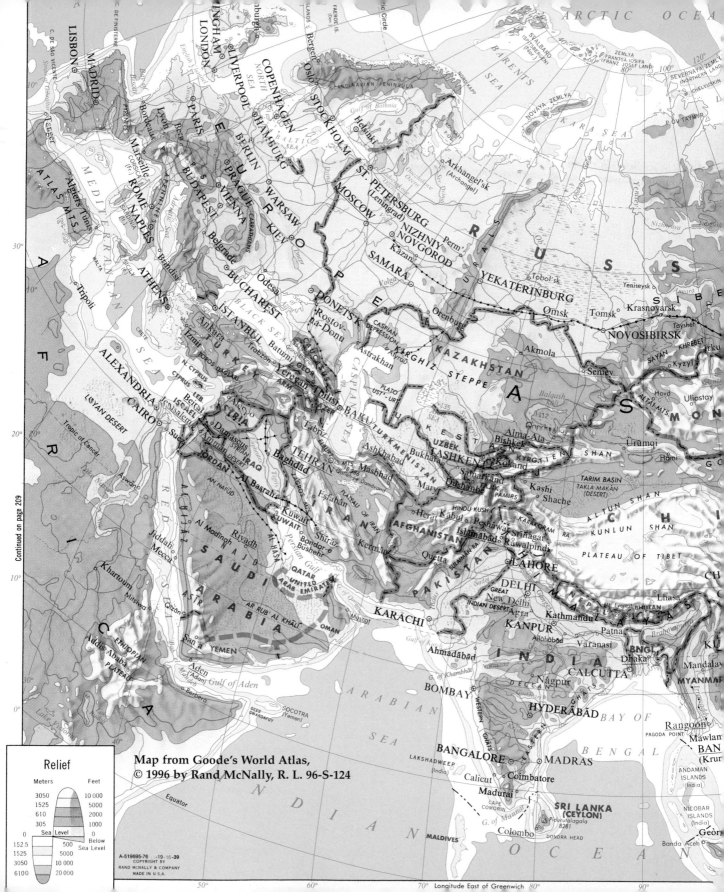

Map from Goode's World Atlas,
© 1996 by Rand McNally, R. L. 96-S-124

Continued on page 209

Relief

Meters		Feet
3050		10 000
1525		5000
610		2000
305		1000
0	Sea Level	0
	Sea Level	Below Sea Level
152.5		500
1525		5000
3050		10 000
6100		20 000

A-519695-76   -19-16-39
COPYRIGHT BY
RAND McNALLY & COMPANY
MADE IN U.S.A.

Longitude East of Greenwich

Map from Cosmopolitan World Atlas,
©1996 Rand McNally, R. L. 96-S124

Enchantment of the World

AFGHANISTAN

By Leila Merrell Foster

Consultant for Afghanistan: Nancy Newell, Research Associate for the University of Nebraska at Omaha; co-author, *The Struggle for Afghanistan*

CHILDREN'S PRESS®
A Division of Grolier Publishing
New York • London • Hong Kong • Sydney
Danbury, Connecticut

The snow-capped Hindu Kush mountains contrast sharply with the dry, dusty plain below.

Project Editor and Design: Jean Blashfield Black
Photo Research: Jay Mallin

Library of Congress Cataloging-in-Publication Data

Foster, Leila Merrell.
  Afghanistan / by Leila Merrell Foster.
    p. cm. -- (Enchantment of the World)
  Includes index.
  Summary: An introduction to the geography, history, culture, and people of Afghanistan, a mountainous country in south-central Asia.
    ISBN 0-516-20017-8
    1. Afghanistan--Juvenile literature. [1. Afghanistan.]
I. Title. II. Series.
DS351.5.F67 1996
958.1--dc20   96-5150
                                                  CIP
                                                  AC

PHOTO CREDITS: ©: Alan Kelso pp. 33, 97 bottom right; AP/Wide World Photos: p. 72; Aramco World Magazine: p. 43, 96 right; Archive Photos: pp. 25, 34, 40; Art Resource: pp. 27, 30 (both photos Borromeo), 22 (Giraudon), 18 bottom (SEF); Bettmann Archive: pp. 21, 41; Black Star: pp. 93 (Charles Crowell), 86, 92 (both photos Christopher Morris), 100 center right, 107 (both photos Klaus Reisinger), 75 (Sean Sutton); Bridgeman Art Library: pp. 18 top, 28, 39; Corbis-Bettmann: p. 37 left; Culver Pictures: p. 46; Gamma-Liaison: pp. 5 (Frederique Lengaigne/GLM), 57 right (Joe Gaal), 106, 109 (both photos Reza), 12, 66, 70, 74 right, 78, 79, 82 left, 103 bottom, 104 (all photos Robert Nickelsberg), 61 (Vlastimir Shone); Historic Royal Palaces: p. 37 right; Impact Visuals: pp. 38, 95, 100 top right, 108 bottom (all photos Alexander Contos); Kate Bader: pp. 17, 49; Luke Powell: pp. 8 right, 8 left, 9, 31, 88, 90 left, 94; Magnum Photos: pp. 73 right, 73 left (both photos Abbas), 83 (C. Steele-Perkins), 81 (Eve Arnold), 98 bottom (Marc Riboud), 13, 56, 57 left, 64 right, 64 left, 68, 91, 102, (all photos Steve McCurry); North Wind Picture Archives: p. 42; P. Hurlin: p. 16 right; Photo Researchers: 16 left (Jean-Michel Labat/JACANA), 97 top, 100 top left (both photos Marcello Bertinetti); Reuters/Bettmann: p. 50; Sovfoto/Eastfoto: pp. 44, 47, 52, 53, 59, 82 right, 57 center right (CTK), 58 (Novosti), 77 bottom left (Tass); Streano/Havens: pp. 4, 6, 10, 67, 69, 80 left, 89, 100 center left, 100 bottom left, 100 bottom right, 103 top, 105, 108 top (all photos Mac Madenwald); Superstock, Inc.: pp. 11, 14 top right, 15, 77 top left, 77 bottom right, 84, 90 right, 96 left, 97 bottom left; Trip: pp. 63, 76 (both photos Trip), 77 top left (A. Dalton), 14 lower left (M. Jenkin), 98 top (M. Lines), 14 top left (Richard Drury), 74 left, 80 right (both photos V. Kolpakov); UPI/Bettmann: pp. 45, 55; Visuals Unlimited: pp. 17 left (Charles Rushing), 20 (A. J. Copley), 87 (Emily Stong).

COVER PHOTO: Bamian Valley.

Several children from a rural area of Afghanistan take time out from their chores to be photographed.

TABLE OF CONTENTS

Afghanistan has a varied landscape, featuring high, rough mountains, fertile valleys, and desertlike plains. Although many areas have been made treeless by people looking for fuelwood, some forests still exist.

Chapter 1

MOUNTAIN STRONGHOLD

What country is known for its fierce fighters and a hoard of ancient gold? What nation has been both a barrier and a highway to conquerors through the ages? From where did the Soviet Union retreat in the 1980s? Afghanistan is the answer to these questions.

A mountainous country in south-central Asia, Afghanistan has a strategic location on both north-south and east-west trade routes. This location has always attracted outsiders, from Alexander the Great in the fourth century B.C. to the Soviet Union in the 1980s.

The people of Afghanistan, called Afghans, include people of many heritages and languages living in thirty-one provinces. After the Soviet forces left in 1989, the Afghans had the task of putting together a government under which all groups could live.

Afghanistan occupies an area of 251,773 square miles (652,089 square kilometers). It is a little smaller than the state of Texas. The Afghan population is estimated at between 15 and 18 million.

The country has no direct access to the sea. The nearest coast is about 300 miles (483 kilometers) to the south along the Arabian Sea. Afghanistan's longest boundary is with Pakistan, located both to the east and to the south. That border is about 1,125 miles (1,810 kilometers) long. To the north, Afghanistan touches the

Tashkurgan (above) lies in the northern foothills of the Hindu Kush mountain range, which stretches across central Afghanistan. The rolling northern plains (right) lead to the Amu Darya River.

republics of Turkmenistan, Uzbekistan, and Tajikistan, all of which were part of the Soviet Union until 1991. Iran lies to the west. The shortest border (50 miles; 80 kilometers) is at the end of the long, narrow Wakhan Corridor in the northeast, touching the People's Republic of China.

THE LAND DIVIDED IN THREE PARTS

Mountains divide the country into three distinct geographic regions. The great mountain range known as the Hindu Kush (meaning "Hindu killer") separates the rich, fertile northern provinces from the rest of the country. The Hindu Kush is linked by that branch of the Himalayas called the Pamirs in Tajikistan to the northeast. The highest peaks in the Hindu Kush are approximately 19,500 to 23,000 feet (6,000 to 7,000 meters). Farther west

Even the southwestern plateau, such as this region in Qandahar Province, is rimmed by high mountains.

around Kabul, the capital, the peaks range from 14,750 to 19,500 feet (4,500 to 6,000 meters) high. Then about 100 miles (161 kilometers) north of Kabul, the mountain range spreads out in a fan shape that creates further divisions of the countryside.

The Hindu Kush and smaller ranges divide the country into three quite different sections: the central highlands, the northern plains, and the southwestern plateau. The central highlands area of about 160,000 square miles (414,000 square kilometers) contains tall peaks and deep, narrow valleys.

North of the central highlands is an area of about 40,000 square miles (103,600 square kilometers) with plains and fertile foothills that slope gently toward the Amu Darya River, which forms the northern border. In the past, that river was called the Oxus. The Amu Darya separates Afghanistan's northern plains from the much larger central Asian highlands of the Pamirs. The average elevation of the northern plains is only about 2,000 feet (610 meters). The region is agricultural and heavily populated. It also boasts some rich mineral resources and natural gas.

The Tarnak River waters a fertile plain in the Qandahar region.

South of the central highlands is the southwestern plateau. With an average elevation of about 3,000 feet (914 meters) and an area of some 50,000 square miles (130,000 square kilometers), the region contains high plateaus, sandy deserts, and semideserts. The Rigestan Desert covers about one-fourth of this section. Several major rivers cross the southwestern plateau, including the Helmand and the Arghandab.

RIVERS AND LAKES

Most of the water in Afghanistan drains within the country, with only an eastern river reaching the ocean. The Kabul River flows into the Indus River, which flows to the Arabian Sea, part of the Indian Ocean. The Amu Darya eventually empties into the Aral Sea. Most of the other rivers rise in the central mountains and empty into inland lakes or dry up in desert sands. Other major rivers include the Kunduz, which runs to the Amu Darya, and the Harirud, which runs through western Afghanistan and Herat.

This small but intriguing lake of the Band-e Amir in the central highlands is fed by a river that creates a narrow, green valley.

The Helmand stretches 900 miles (1,448 kilometers) from mountains about 50 miles (80 kilometers) west of Kabul, through the desert, until it reaches the marshes and the lake region. The river remains relatively salt-free for much of its length, unlike most rivers with no outlet to the sea. This river basin offers good potential for irrigation and increased agriculture.

Though Afghanistan has few large lakes, five small lakes in the central highlands known as Band-e Amir are famous for their unusual coloring, from milky-white to dark green. The underlying

Although most of Afghanistan has a dry or semidry climate, precipitation and the warm temperatures of spring can make Kabul's gardens bloom.

bedrock causes the color difference. The Hamun-e Saberi is a brackish marsh where flamingos breed.

CLIMATE

Afghanistan has very cold winters and hot, dry summers. Arnold Toynbee, a famous historian, described the climate of Afghanistan as like a Turkish bath, with the chilly room at the high elevations above 7,000 feet (2,134 meters) and the steam room at 3,000 feet (914 meters) and below.

In addition to the variation that elevation changes bring, the weather is affected by the movement of air masses and precipitation that blows against the tall mountains. The higher mountains

The bitter winter weather in the high mountains made fleeing to safety in Pakistan treacherous for refugees from war-torn Afghanistan.

of the northeast have a subarctic climate with dry, cold winters, while the mountains along the Pakistan border are affected by the Indian *monsoons* (rain-bearing winds) that occur between July and September. In the southwest, humid air from the Persian Gulf occasionally brings showers and thunderstorms during the summer.

Cold air masses in winter from the north and northwest bring snow and bitter cold to the highlands and rain at lower elevations. The *mujahideen*, Afghan guerrilla fighters who fought against the Soviet Union, called the hailstones that fell in the mountains "Allah's minesweepers" because the force of the ice pellets was often strong enough to set off the land mines planted by the Soviet army.

The wide temperature range has included a reading of 120° Fahrenheit (48.8° C) in Jalalabad in July and –24° F. (–31°C) at Kabul in the winter.

Precipitation also occurs in extremes, with the most in the east and the least in the west. At the Salang Pass of the Hindu Kush, a record annual precipitation of 53 inches (135 centimeters) was

Careful tending of forestland (above) is an important activity for ensuring the country's future. Hawthorn trees (above left) and honeysuckle bushes (left) are among the colorful woody plants that grow in areas with enough water.

recorded. In the arid region of Farah in the west, only 3 inches (8 centimeters) a year were recorded. Most of the precipitation falls from December to April. During summer, Afghans experience hot, dry, cloudless weather everywhere except in the monsoon areas.

PLANTS

With such a range of climate and terrain, Afghanistan has a great variety of plant life. Arctic and alpine flora thrive at high altitudes while salt-tolerant, arid-zone plants live in the deserts.

Trees grow in some areas, but much of Afghanistan's timber supply has been cut for fuel. Large forest trees, such as pine and

A juniper tree gains a look of mystery at sunset.

fir, remain primarily in the high mountains. Some grow as tall as 180 feet (55 meters). Most of the fir trees grow at altitudes above 10,000 feet (3,048 meters). Cedars frequently grow between 5,500 feet (1,676 meters) and 7,200 feet (2,195 meters). Below that, oak, walnut, alder, ash, and juniper trees are present. Shrubs such as rose, honeysuckle, hawthorn, currant, and gooseberry may be found. In the early spring, rains bring on flowering grasses and herbs in some areas that seem lifeless the rest of the year.

ANIMALS

Wild animals favoring a harsh habitat live in Afghanistan. Large mammals have practically disappeared, fallen to the guns of hunting Afghans. The Siberian tiger used to be found along the banks of the Amu Darya. Wolves, foxes, hyenas, and jackals still live in the mountains, while gazelles, wild dogs, and wild cats are common. Wild goats include the markhor, with its long, twisted horns, and the ibex, which has long, backward-curving horns. Wild sheep, such as the urial and argali, range the Pamirs and the Hindu Kush. Bears live in the mountains and forest. Smaller

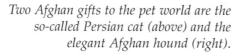

Two Afghan gifts to the pet world are the so-called Persian cat (above) and the elegant Afghan hound (right).

mammals include the mongoose, mole, shrew, hedgehog, bat, and several species of kangaroo rats, or jerboas.

Several of Afghanistan's domesticated animals have become famous. A Chinese emperor once sent for a supply of Badakhshani horses. Because of the horses' reputation for speed and endurance, he wanted them for his army. Afghanistan is also the home of the cat that was incorrectly named "Persian." The tall, elegant Afghan hound has become popular in the West.

Sheep, cattle, and goats are important meat and dairy sources for the Afghans, who frequently move their animals up and down the mountainsides with the seasons. Sheep are the most important food animals. Camels, donkeys, and horses are used for transport.

Mountain streams teem with trout and salmon, and sturgeon can be caught in the Amu Darya. However, while Afghans love hunting, they are not fond of fishing.

The markhor (left) of the Himalayas and nearby mountains is one of five species of wild goats. Nomads with their versatile camels (above) are a common sight in Afghanistan.

Several birds of prey, such as vultures and eagles, find a home in Afghanistan. Migrating birds are plentiful during the spring and fall seasons. Pheasants, quails, cranes, pelicans, snipes, partridges, and crows are common.

SETTLEMENT PATTERNS

Given the differences in land and climate and the strategic land routes through Afghanistan, it is not surprising that a variety of people have settled there. They have retained their different ways of life. The nation is a mosaic—not a melting pot—of people.

Mountain and desert regions are sparsely settled. Farmers and nomads are distributed unevenly. Most of the people are in oases or fertile valleys. The larger towns are located along the major circular road.

There are two major language groups, each with many dialects. Often Afghans find it difficult to communicate with people from other areas. The common language of business is Afghan Persian, which they call *Dari*.

Left: This gold griffin necklace from the treasure found along the Oxus River (Amu Darya), was created during the Achaemenid Empire, which existed from 500 to 400 B.C.

Below: A carved wall at the palace at Persepolis (in present-day Iran) once graced the seat of the Achaemenid kings.

Chapter 2

ANCIENT TREASURE

"Gold!" Surely the discovery of golden crowns and jewels would delight archeologists studying ancient civilizations. In fact, while such treasures reveal information about the art of the past, they may not tell as much as pottery or clay tablets with writing.

Soviet archeologists at the site of the Tillya-Tepe dig in 1978 silently cursed their find of gold because of the extra work it made for them. Victor Sarianidi, the archeologist in charge, told how the members of his team wished that they were dealing with pieces of clay pots. They could then leave the pieces lying handy around their work, because nobody thought they were valuable. But when working with gold, they had to count carefully each piece after they worked with it. And they did not like having to use armed guards to prevent theft of the gold.

Several important treasures have been unearthed in Afghanistan because of the country's location on ancient trade routes. Archeologists are just at the beginning of their discoveries. They can expect to make significant finds in the future.

PREHISTORY

Before 1950, information about early humans in Afghanistan was almost unknown. At that time, Carleton S. Coon, then of the

Lapis lazuli, the semi-precious blue stone, was an early trade item in Afghanistan.

University of Pennsylvania, began the first archeological survey to identify prehistoric sites. Louis B. Dupree, a major scholar in Afghan studies, and others became involved in cave explorations.

Based on these investigations, scientists believe that humans lived in Afghanistan as early as 100,000 B.C. A cave at Darra-i-Kur in Badakhshan (a province in present-day Afghanistan) produced a Neanderthal skull fragment—that is, a bone section from an early human head—and tools that probably date to thirty thousand years ago. Other caves near Aq Kopruk contained evidence of a culture based on domesticated animals from about 9000 to 6000 B.C. More recent sites, from about 3000 to 2000 B.C., have also been identified. Because of the presence of wild strains of wheat and barley, Afghanistan should be studied to help us understand how humans began cultivating crops and domesticating animals.

During this early period, trade existed between Afghanistan and Egypt and Mesopotamia to the west. Mesopotamia included parts of present-day Syria, Turkey, and Iraq. Afghans supplied lapis lazuli, a valuable blue stone, that was mined in Badakhshan. Also, a site has been excavated that shows links of the Afghans with a civilization to the southeast along the Indus River, which flows through Pakistan.

THE ACHAEMENID EMPIRE

The historical record of Afghanistan is ancient. Some scholars suggest that the Afghan landscape is mentioned in the hymns of *Rig Veda*, the Sanskrit source of Hinduism established around 1000 B.C. by people who migrated into India. Others claim that the first mention is in the *Avesta*, teachings of Zarathustra, the religious leader who lived around 500 B.C. and influenced the Achaemenid Empire, which included Afghanistan.

Much uncertainty exists about the life of Zarathustra, but most historians agree that he was killed in or near Balkh in northern Afghanistan around 522 B.C. during an invasion of nomads from central Asia. Zarathustra taught a religion, often called Parsee, that concerned the conflict of Good with Evil for control of the universe. He believed that humans can help Good through good thoughts, words, and deeds.

Darius I, king of Persia about 500 B.C., followed Zarathustra's teachings. Darius became the head of the

Zarathustra, or Zoroaster, was a religious leader in early Afghanistan.

Achaemenid Empire, which had been founded by Achaemenes, a local king who had been able to extend his reign over a large area. Darius expanded the empire from part of Afghanistan to the Mediterranean, including Egypt.

The Behistun Rock in present-day Iran contains a stone relief carving of Darius I with rebels he had conquered. In three languages, the stone lists the countries in Darius's empire. The list includes territory now in Afghanistan.

The empire had a remarkable government that encouraged trade and built roads and irrigation systems. It used Aramaic as the language for official business, and it is from Aramaic that local script was developed in Afghanistan. Beautiful gold and silver jewelry and vessels from the fifth century B.C. found near the Oxus River—thus called the Oxus Treasure—reflect the lavish lifestyle. Carvings in the ruins of the palace at Persepolis (in present-day Iran) show the power of this empire.

ALEXANDER THE GREAT

The destruction of the Achaemenid Empire came from the west. Between 336 and 330 B.C., Alexander the Great, the son of Philip II of Macedonia, swept in and destroyed the empire and conquered the Afghan provinces. According to the historians of that time, Bactrian cavalry, from the area called Balkh in present-day Afghanistan, were among the greatest fighters opposing Alexander.

Alexander used speed and daring to outmaneuver the armies of central Asia. Alexander marched his troops over snowy mountain passes. He had them cross rivers in animal-skin boats or leather tents turned into rafts. He built a number of cities named after himself, including Alexandria, Egypt.

In 327 B.C. Alexander was fighting guerrillas near Derbent on the Caspian Sea north of Iran. When Alexander demanded that the guerrillas surrender, they told him he would need to use "winged soldiers," pointing out that their stronghold was unconquerable because it was surrounded by sheer, snowcapped cliffs.

Alexander called for three hundred volunteers to scale the cliffs with ropes and iron pegs, promising three hundred gold pieces to each one who reached the top. Although thirty fell to their death, the other men reached the top under cover of darkness. The next morning when the guerrillas saw Alexander's soldiers standing on the cliffs above them, they surrendered.

Among the prisoners taken was a beautiful woman named Roxane. Afghan folktales say that Alexander fell in love with her but would not force himself on her as other conquerors might have done. Her father, impressed with this courtesy and certainly aware of the political advantages, became Alexander's ally.

Roxane and Alexander were married in a ceremony and feast at which the bride was handed a ritual piece of bread sliced with her bridegroom's sword. By eating her piece of the bridal loaf, she accepted Alexander. After the wedding, Alexander was campaigning for most of the five years before his death. He died before the son she bore him was born.

That this match was based on love rather than politics seems probable since a marriage with the daughter of Darius would have been more useful than a wedding with the daughter of a local chief. Indeed, Alexander later married the princess of the family of Darius in an elaborate ceremony in which many of his generals joined in taking wives of high-born women of the Achaemenid Empire. Roxane probably arranged to have the princess killed after Alexander's death. Later, Roxane and her son were also murdered, leaving Alexander with no heirs.

In Afghanistan, girls are still named Roxane. Alexander is known as *Iskander* in the Afghan languages. Chiefs claim descent from Alexander. Mighty horses are said to be descended from Alexander's great steed, Bucephalus.

After Alexander's death in 323 B.C., his empire split into three sections with Seleucus, one of his generals, taking the eastern section that included Afghanistan. At the great mass marriage feast of Alexander's army, Seleucus had been given the daughter of a dead guerrilla chief who had lived under Alexander's protection. Unlike others married at that time, Seleucus did not abandon his wife after Alexander's death, and she became his queen and the founder of their dynasty.

The Seleucids ruled from a capital at Babylon. About 304 B.C.,

An artist's idea of Alexander the Great visiting the tent where the captive family of King Darius III was being held.

the territory to the south of the Hindu Kush was given to a dynasty of kings who ruled in northern India. Some Afghan rock inscriptions in Greek and Aramaic date from the reign of Asoka, the best known of these kings.

Later, around 250 B.C., a local Greek ruler in Bactria declared the Afghan plain south of the Amu Darya independent. By

180 B.C., the Greco-Bactrian forces had established their rule near Kabul and in the Punjab in India. The Parthians in eastern Iran also broke away from the Seleucids and took over some parts of southern Afghanistan.

THE KUSHANS

About 135 B.C., five central Asian tribes joined together under the leadership of one of these tribes, known as the Kushan, to drive the Greeks out of Bactria. Kushan rule was extended from north-central India as far as the frontiers of China.

During the Kushan period, one of the great trading routes of history, the Silk Road linking China with Rome, passed through Afghanistan with a transfer center at Balkh. Ideas, as well as luxury goods, passed along the route. Buddhist architecture, art—including a giant figuresculpted into a hillside—and beliefs were spread throughout Afghanistan.

North of Kabul, archeologists digging up the remains of the old Silk Road have recovered painted glass from Alexandria, bronze and alabaster from Rome, carved ivory from India, and lacquer from China. New discoveries of golden objects help to fill in an understanding of this period.

THE SASSANIANS AND HEPHTHALITES

While the Kushans governed in Afghanistan, another group of people called the Parthians controlled most of the Iranian plateau in the west. Several of the tribes from that region held on to their Zoroastrian religion by moving into the mountains. As the

This detail from a wall painting from the Kushan period in Kakrak, Afghanistan, shows a close view of Buddha. The people of the Kushan tribes brought Buddhism to Afghanistan, though it was later overwhelmed by Islam.

Kushan empire crumbled, these tribes emerged as the Sassanians. From A.D. 241 to about 400, the Sassanians established control in Afghanistan. However, some of that control was in name only, with the Kushan leaders exercising the real power. This was a period of nationalistic reaction against Greek, Roman, and central Asian influences. Along the Silk Road, this reaction took the form of attacks on caravans, so many merchants began to move their goods on ships.

In A.D. 400, a new wave of nomads, the Hephthalites, came out of central Asia. They conquered about thirty semi-independent kingdoms. They held power only until 565 when they were defeated by the Sassanians and western Turks.

In the seventh century, Arab armies attacked the Sassanian Empire. They brought with them the religion of Islam and a new era for Afghanistan.

بنينه رن لوكليكيحيتاى رعفت ومحبت يدن وسيون رسين لوكليكيحيتان بابرليرينهيدى
اغاحتلابلاين اماليان ارعقان ديوان يرعان لهين يجوانماس لهين نكيتانتاين اليلالان لبابريد يعين
شغلان ديوحقيمهتان يلب يبيهتان اعزيم ملعقيهجن لهكليكيحين لغلفتان ابلادان ايهان رعول اينهين بجوان
تشنبرتختى ترى الدين يرعان لهكليكيحيمل بنى بسين لوكليكيحيتان بابرليرينهين بابرليرينهيدى

Chapter 3

MUSLIM DYNASTIES

Under the Hephthalites and Sassanians, many of the Afghan rulers were Hindus, or they worshiped in temples that contained both Hindu and Buddhist statues, indicating a mingling of these two religions. Then from the west came the Arabs, bringing with them a third religion, Islam. The Arabs defeated the Sassanians and occupied Afghan land. After the eighth century, Islamic—often called Muslim—rulers would hold power.

EARLY ISLAMIC DYNASTIES

At first, Muslim conquest of the Afghan territory lacked depth. The people would convert to Islam when the Arab armies were present, but when the armies moved on, the people would go back to their old ways of doing things.

In the beginning, some of the Afghan rulers were under the power of the Arabs who had their base in Damascus (in present-day Syria). Then other Arabs with a different idea of how the leader should be chosen took over power and established their capital at Baghdad (in Iraq). Local revolts took place throughout

Left: An illustration for a thirteenth-century Persian book shows the great conqueror, Genghis Khan, in his tent, surrounded by his soldiers and aides.

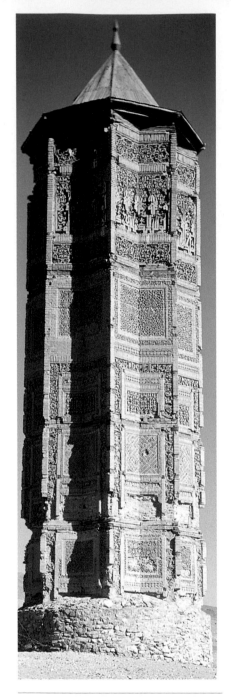

This highly carved stone tower was built in Ghazni during the eleventh century.

the Islamic world. A strong Muslim leader at Baghdad was able to consolidate power into the Abbasid Empire during his reign from 754 to 775. However, by 850 the Abbasid Empire was crumbling in the east.

In Afghan territory, local rulers went their own way, giving only formal allegiance to Baghdad. In the areas of Bukhara and Samarkand, both northeast of present-day Afghanistan, different groups held power for short periods of time. Balkh came under the domination of the Samanids of Persia from 872 to 999. This was a golden age of learning and art, with the Samanid cities rivaling Baghdad.

In the tenth century, the Turks of Turkestan to the north conquered the Samanids. Several former Turkish slaves seized power. One seized the area around Kabul and east as far as the Indus River. Then his son, Mahmud of Ghazni, came to power in 998 and conquered the Punjab, in what is now India, and converted many Hindus to Islam. Mahmud built a strong Sunni Muslim dynasty that prevented the Shiite Muslims in Persia from spreading.

Mahmud turned his capital, Ghazni, into a center of learning. Among the nine hundred scholars who were brought to

These ruins are all that remain of the city of Farah, destroyed by Genghis Khan and his Mongol army almost eight centuries ago.

the court were al-Biruni, a scientist and historian; Firdausi, a poet; and al-Utbi, another historian. Art flourished in the city.

With the death of Mahmud, the power of the dynasty declined. The citizens of Ghazni were defeated by people from the city of Ghor in central Afghanistan. Their rulers were driven into India. The people from Ghor were overwhelmed by a new wave of Turks, who ruled from the borders of Chinese Turkistan to Iraq.

THE MONGOLS

For the next centuries, Afghanistan was most often under the rule of invaders from the east. In 1219, Genghis, called *Khan,* meaning "supreme ruler," and his army charged in from Mongolia. The Mongols killed without mercy and destroyed cities and their civilizations. They let the canals fill up with sediment, harming transportation and commerce. They destroyed fine books and other art treasures.

When the Afghans challenged him, Genghis Khan laid siege to

the forts and palaces of Bamian in central Afghanistan. When Genghis Khan's grandson was killed in the fighting, he ordered every person and animal in the city and the city itself to be destroyed.

The Mongols also tried to destroy Islam, but they were unable to do so. In fact, the Great Khan's own great-grandson eventually became a devout Muslim and tried to restore Islamic culture.

After the death of Genghis Khan, his empire began to disintegrate. In Afghanistan, some local chiefs were independent and others acknowledged an allegiance to a Mongol ruler. Then, at the end of the fourteenth century, came another invader.

THE TIMURID PERIOD

Timur, also known as Tamerlane, and his mighty army of horsemen rode in from the north, where they had established a capital at Samarkand. They conquered much of the Afghan territory on the way to building an empire that stretched from India to Turkey. Absolutely ruthless in killing his enemies, Timur became famous for building towers from the skulls of people he had defeated. However, during the later period of Timurid rule, Afghanistan went through a golden time of peace and prosperity.

Timur's successors in the Persian area made their capital at Herat in Afghanistan. There they constructed buildings filled with art treasures and turned the city into a center of scholarship boasting such poets as Jami and such artists as Bihzad. A Persian architect, Qavam-ud-Din, constructed a combination place of worship and school. The Timurids in Herat were conquered about 1507 by Muhammad Shaybani Khan, leader of the Uzbek Turks, and from his time on the Uzbeks settled in Afghanistan.

These ruins of an ancient fortress overlook the city of Herat, which was already old when the Timurid kings made it their capital.

MOGULS AND SAFAVIDS

Between 1500 and 1747, Afghanistan was the target of two feuding empires, the Persian Safavid dynasty to the west and the Muslim Indian Mogul dynasty to the south and east. By that time, the horsemanship for which the Mongols had been famous had become less important because the fighters had acquired gunpowder.

Babur, a young military genius whose name means "tiger," was the founder of the Mogul dynasty. Descended from Timur on his father's side and from Genghis Khan on his mother's, he ruled his father's province in Ferghana in present-day Uzbekistan from age twelve. Two years later he conquered Samarkand, but he was driven from both Samarkand and Ferghana when he was eighteen. At twenty-one he led his troops across the Hindu Kush and captured Afghanistan.

Babur used Afghanistan as a base for attacking India, and in

1526 he marched into India with a small but effective force of 12,000 fighters, who destroyed an army of 100,000. Babur made Agra in India his capital, but all eastern Afghanistan up to the Hindu Kush was part of his empire. When Babur died in 1530, he was buried in his favorite garden in Kabul.

Babur, founder of the Mogul dynasty in India, incorporated Afghanistan into his empire.

With the death of Babur, Afghanistan became a pawn in the contest between the Mogul empire of India and the Safavid empire of Iran, which controlled most of western Afghanistan. For two centuries, boundaries shifted frequently and the major cities changed hands. But in the country-side, at least 345 separate tribal units held power.

THE HOTAKIS

In 1709, Mir Wais Khan, a leader in the Hotaki Ghilzai tribe, successfully led an uprising against Gurgin Khan, the Safavid governor who had been brutally suppressing the tribe. Mir Wais's political tactics illustrate an important division among the Afghan people and among Muslims as a whole. The Safavid Persians were Shiite Muslims, while Mir Wais was a Sunni Muslim. (This division in Islam arose in the years immediately following the Prophet Muhammad's death.)

When Mir Wais made his pilgrimage to Mecca, he secured a *fatwa,* a religious statement, which proclaimed that a Sunni revolt against a heretical Shiite ruler was a righteous act. This document encouraged others to revolt against the Shiite leader.

Mir Wais never claimed he was king, but he took the title of *vakil,* or "governor." After the death of Mir Wais, his son, Mir Mahmud, seized power from his uncle, and attacked and overthrew the Safavid ruler. Mahmud turned out to be a cruel ruler, murdering thousands to strengthen his power and becoming mentally unbalanced. In 1725, Mahmud was murdered by his army, and Ashraf, a young cousin, was put in power.

Ashraf beat back the Russians from the north and the Ottoman Turks in the west. However, he was as cruel as his cousin. An outlaw chief, Nadir Quli, attacked and defeated Ashraf. Ashraf was murdered, probably on orders from a cousin.

NADIR SHAH

Nadir Quli was born a poor man who worked his way into power as the head of a band of outlaws in a section of Persia, or Iran, called Khurasan. He consolidated his forces there and then marched on Herat in 1732. When that city fell, he received many of its soldiers into his own army because he was impressed with their courage. In 1736, he was elected *shah,* or "supreme ruler," of Persia. In Afghanistan, Nadir Shah seized Qandahar, then Kabul and Ghazni and advanced into India. He defeated the Moguls in 1739 at Karnal, north of Delhi. He took the treasures of the Moguls, including the Koh-i-noor diamond and the Peacock Throne, and returned to Persia. He also claimed three hundred elephants, ten thousand horses, and ten thousand camels.

Nadir then made conquests in present-day Uzbekistan and returned to Mashhad in Iran, which he made his capital. Nadir Shah became increasingly suspicious of others. He blinded his own son, whom he thought wanted to seize power. He killed great numbers of people until he himself was beheaded in 1747.

THE DURRANI DYNASTY

Ahmad Khan Abdali, the Afghan leader of Nadir Shah's personal bodyguards, left Mashhad with four thousand soldiers, taking with him much of the personal treasury, including the Koh-i-noor diamond. He was elected chief of the Abdali tribe, taking the titles *Ahmad Shah* and *Durr-i-durran*, meaning "pearl of pearls."

Ahmad Shah succeeded in winning the respect of many other tribal leaders in Afghanistan and extending his empire from Meshed and Delhi in India and from the Amu Darya to the Arabian Sea. In the second half of the eighteenth century, Ahmad Shah ruled the second greatest Muslim Empire, surpassed only by the Ottomans centered in present-day Turkey. Ahmad Shah's popularity as a national hero and his large family won him the title of *baba,* or "father."

Among the fabled treasures that have passed through the hands of Afghanistan's kings are the Peacock Throne of Persia (left) and the huge Koh-i-noor diamond, now in one of the Royal Crowns of England (shown above in the right-hand crown).

Ahmad Shah died in 1772 and was succeeded by his son, Timur Shah. The son, kept busy putting down rebellions, changed his capital from Qandahar to Kabul in 1776 and died in 1793.

The fifth son of Timur Shah, Zaman, seized the throne and turned his attention to an advance into India. Under urging from the British in India, the Persian shah provided men and money to Mahmud, a brother of Zaman, to capture Qandahar. Successful, Mahmud pushed on toward Kabul, thereby forcing his brother to return from India. Zaman was captured and handed over to Mahmud, who had him blinded and imprisoned.

The Durrani Empire had begun to disintegrate after 1798 when Zaman had appointed Ranjit Singh, a Sikh, not a Muslim, as governor of the province of Lahore. By then, Great Britain had become a major player in the area.

The Khyber Pass is a narrow gap at an altitude of 3,500 feet (1,067 meters) through the Safid Kuh mountains of the Hindu Kush. One of the main routes from central Asia into India, it has been of strategic importance since ancient times. It became world famous in 1842 during the First Anglo-Afghan War.

Chapter 4

THE GREAT GAME

The strategic location of Afghanistan for both the defense and the conquest of the Indian subcontinent aroused the attention of foreign nations. As Europeans explored the world and discovered profitable sea routes for trade with Asia, new players arrived on the Afghan scene.

The British had begun their involvement in India in 1600 when Queen Elizabeth I granted a charter for the East India Company to trade in that region. By the middle of the eighteenth century, the French, Portuguese, and Dutch were competing with the British for trade and political influence.

Since the time of Peter the Great in the early 1700s, tsarist Russia had been looking for warm-water ports with outlets on the Mediterranean Sea, Persian Gulf (part of the Arabian Sea), or Indian Ocean. Russia expanded east across Siberia, reached the Pacific Ocean, and pushed across the Bering Strait into Alaska and California. But it also moved

The coat of arms of the East India Company. It opened up India and central Asia for Britain.

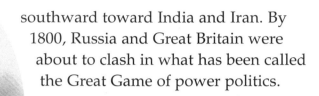

southward toward India and Iran. By 1800, Russia and Great Britain were about to clash in what has been called the Great Game of power politics.

OPENING PLAYS OF THE GAME

Fearing the threat of a Franco-Russian invasion of India in 1809, the British concluded a treaty with Shah Shoja of the Durrani dynasty to oppose passage of foreign troops through Afghan territory. Shortly after the British left Peshawar, where the treaty had been made, Shah Shoja was overthrown.

Dost Muhammad

Dost Muhammad, son of the founder of the powerful Barakzai dynasty in Afghanistan, emerged as the leader. He took the title of *amir,* meaning "chief," in 1826 at Kabul. When he lost Peshawar, Afghanistan's former capital, to the Sikh ruler of the Punjab area of India, the Dost began a fight that he was destined to lose.

In 1836, Dost Muhammad declared a *jihad,* an Islamic holy war, and gathered an army to attack the Sikh leader, Ranjit Singh, who shrewdly set one faction of Dost Muhammad's forces against the other. The army fell apart, and Peshawar was permanently lost to the Afghans.

From the west, Muhammad Shah of Persia attacked Herat in November 1837. Because Russia supported the Persians, the British became alarmed that the Russians might use Afghanistan as their gateway into India. The British established alliances with Afghan rulers in Herat, Kabul, and Qandahar. Dost Muhammad welcomed the British if they would help him win Peshawar back. The British would not give this promise, and Dost started talking to a Russian agent in Kabul. The British used this as an excuse to invade Afghanistan.

Then followed the First Anglo-Afghan War, from 1839 to 1842, in which the British succeeded in capturing Kabul but were forced to retreat at the cost of thousands of lives. Though Dost Muhammad temporarily lost power to Shoja, he regained the throne when the British withdrew. Over the next twenty years until his death in 1862, Dost Muhammad consolidated his power over most of Afghanistan, but he never regained Peshawar.

The Second Anglo-Afghan War, lasting from 1878 to 1880, occurred after many years of disagreements between the new amir, Sher Ali Khan, the third son of Dost Muhammad, and the British.

A painting records British soldiers at the Battle of Maiwand, Afghanistan, in 1880 in the Second Anglo-Afghan War. Many artists and writers, including Rudyard Kipling, found the place and times romantic.

Abdur Rahman Khan

When Sher Ali allowed a Russian delegation into Kabul but refused to see the British, the British invaded Afghanistan. After Sher Ali died in 1879, his son, Yaqub, signed an agreement to let Britain dictate Afghan foreign affairs. Then he abdicated and went into exile.

Abdur Rahman Khan, a nephew of Sher Ali, who had been living in central Asia, returned and, with British support, proclaimed himself Amir of Kabul. During his reign from 1880 to 1901, the British and Russians agreed on the boundaries that now shape modern Afghanistan. The Durand Agreement of 1893 with the British established Afghanistan as a buffer between the Russian and the British Indian frontiers. Abdur Rahman established a strong centralized government by fighting about twenty small wars that forced the various tribal groups to cooperate. He was able to designate his eldest son, Habibullah Khan, as his successor without any of the usual challenges by family members at his death in 1901. He preserved the internal independence of his country.

INTO THE TWENTIETH CENTURY

Habibullah Khan, Abdur Rahman's son, ruled from 1901 to 1919. He continued his father's introduction of modern technology and the building of a strong central government. He also changed

This beautiful tomb was built for Abdur Rahman Khan, often egarded as the founder of modern Afghanistan.

the education system by introducing the first secondary school in 1904 and by broadening the traditional religious studies.

During his reign, an Afghan nationalist, Mahmud Beg Tarzi, began publishing a periodical called *Seraj-ul-Akbar*, or "Torch of the News." Tarzi also published a children's journal, *Seraj-ul-Aftal*, "Light of Children," which ran six issues in 1918. Tarzi had political influence beyond Afghanistan. His daughter, Soraya, married Amanullah, Habibullah's third son. Tarzi, Amanullah, and others urged Habibullah to enter World War I on the side of Germany and its allies. Habibullah, who had been impressed with British power, especially during a visit to British India in 1907, resisted and kept Afghanistan neutral. For this he was murdered on February 20, 1919, by persons in the anti-British group.

Amanullah seized power, declared Afghanistan independent, and invaded British India in 1919, triggering the Third Anglo-Afghan War. After a month-long war, the Treaty of Rawalpindi, an Indian city now in Pakistan, was signed. Under the treaty, the

In 1921 the Afghans entered into a treaty of friendship with the Bolshevik regime in the new Soviet Union, becoming the first nation to recognize the Soviet government. Sixty years later, Babrak Karmal, prime minister of Afghanistan, spoke at a meeting celebrating the anniversary of the Soviet-Afghan Friendship Treaty.

Afghans gained the right to conduct their own foreign policy and the British cut off their subsidy of money.

Amanullah's hopes to expand his territory were stopped as neighboring governments strengthened their power. He turned his attention to changing his own government. He changed his title from *amir* to *padshah,* or "king." He introduced the first constitution setting up legislative councils, a new system of courts, and secular codes of laws to replace the tribal codes. Amanullah changed the system of taxes and budgets, and after a trip to Europe in 1927-28, he began a reform of the social system. He advocated the removal of the veil for women and founded coeducational schools.

However, Amanullah had allowed his army to become weak. The reforms sparked opposition from conservative religious and tribal leaders. Uprisings began in the eastern part of the country and spread into a civil war. In 1928, a Tajik bandit-hero called Bacha Saqqao, meaning "Son of a Water Carrier," seized Kabul,

*Amanullah abdicated in 1929
and went to live in Italy.*

proclaiming himself Habibullah
Ghazi II. Amanullah abdicated in
1929 and fled to India and then
on to Europe where he died in
1960 without regaining his power.

THE MUSAHIBAN FAMILY

Habibullah Ghazi II was
driven from the throne within
nine months and was executed by
Mohammed Nadir Shah and his
brothers, who were distant cousins of Amanullah. They were
members of the Musahiban family, descended from a brother of
Dost Muhammad. They had been out of the country because of
disagreements with Amanullah. They returned with the support
of the Pushtun Afghans against the Tajiks.

Mohammad Nadir Shah, the oldest Musahiban brother, was
elected king by a tribal assembly. He immediately strengthened
the army. He began a program of more cautious reform with a
new 1931 constitution based somewhat on the 1923 effort of
Amanullah. The economy improved with several leaders starting
small-scale industrial and trading efforts. Nadir Shah was neutral
toward the Soviet Union and Great Britain while trying to gain
support from the United States and European countries.

This old photograph might have been taken at almost any time in the last hundred years, during one of the many times Afghans fought at the Khyber Pass.

The ruling class argued over the power acquired by the Musahiban family. First a brother and then Nadir were assassinated. His nineteen-year-old son, Zahir Shah, took his father's title in 1933, but the real power lay with the prime minister, an uncle, Hashim.

The Musahiban family pursued a policy of preserving independence while encouraging friendship with foreign countries. Afghanistan was a neutral nation during World War II. Pushtu was adopted as the official language to encourage people of the many different tribes to think of themselves as one people— Afghans—instead of as members of many separate tribes. Nationalism also was encouraged by an educational system that led to opportunities at higher levels and ultimately to the University of Kabul. Improved communications and the growth of newspapers helped people to keep in touch. A bank founded in

1932 and new highways and textile industries were signs of progress.

World War II interrupted some of these trends. Several tribes showed their unhappiness by revolts in 1944 and 1945. Shah Mahmud Khan, the youngest brother of Hashim, took over as prime minister. After the war, a poorly planned program for providing water for a large part of southwestern Afghanistan in the Helmand Valley failed to bring the desired results compared with the cost. Economic difficulties increased.

Newspapers are an important source of information for those Afghans in the cities who can read.

As Afghans began to participate in a democratic system with a parliament, opposition groups sprang up. A movement calling itself "Awakened Youth" began agitating for social reforms. Free elections gave an opportunity for criticism of the government and for passage of laws guaranteeing a free press. Since the backers of these reforms had little support from the rest of the country, the government abandoned its tolerance of criticism and controlled the 1952 election for parliament. However, Afghans had learned of new tools of opposition in a democratic environment.

PUSHTUN UNITY

The Durand Agreement of 1893 had placed many Pushtun people in British India. Then, in 1947, two new independent neighboring nations were created—India and Pakistan. At that time, Afghanistan's relationship with Pakistan heated up over the Pushtun people living on the frontier of Pakistan. The Afghans argued that these people should be given the choice of forming an independent country—Pushtunistan—instead of being forced to join Pakistan or India. Pakistan did not appreciate this idea and closed its borders with Afghanistan. With the trade routes through Pakistan cut off, the Afghans turned to the Soviet Union for help.

In 1953 Shah Mahmud was replaced as prime minister by his nephew, Mohammad Daoud, who stayed in power for the next ten years. Daoud pushed for more modernization, with economic improvements planned and directed by the state. He played the Soviet Union and the West against each other to gain economic support from both. He introduced educational reform and supported voluntary removal of the veil from women and abolishing *purdah*, the practice of keeping women out of public sight. In 1959 the wives and daughters of high officials appeared on a holiday reviewing stand without their veils. The crowds below gazed up in shock. However, Daoud's regime, though reform-minded, tolerated no direct opposition.

The unsolved Pushtunistan problem caused the king, Zahir Shah, to remove Daoud from power in 1963. His resignation helped to open up the borders with Pakistan.

Zahir Shah with his advisors then tried an experiment in constitutional monarchy with a new constitution approved in 1964 by the *Loya Jirgah,* the "Great National Assembly of Notables." Under the new system of government, the *Wolesi Jirgah,* "House of the People," had 216 elected members, and the *Meshrano Jirgah,* "House of the Elders," had 84 members. The elders were chosen

The chaderi, worn by many Muslim women when leaving their homes, is a full veil that covers the head, face, and body.

one-third by vote of the people, one-third by the king, and one-third indirectly chosen by assemblies in the provinces.

Elections were held in 1965 with women voting for the first time. Unofficial political parties represented a range of views from the radical left to the fundamentalist religious right. The government and the Parliament deadlocked on many issues. The king appointed at least five different prime ministers between 1965 and 1972 but refused to adopt several key pieces of legislation designed to allow the political process that was supposedly guaranteed under the constitution. The political situation was made worse by severe droughts in the early 1970s that resulted in enormous loss of life— perhaps as many as 100,000 people died.

Finally, Mohammad Daoud seized power from the king with support from military officers with left-wing ideas and from members of the Parcham, or "Banner," Party. Daoud abolished the 1964 constitution, declared Afghanistan a republic, and took charge as chairman of the Central Committee of the republic and as prime minister. Thus the monarchy came to an end on July 17, 1973, and a new era began.

*This small boy is one of the many victims of the long years of fighting in Afghanistan.
His home in Asadabad and his family were destroyed during the civil war.*

Chapter 5

A REPUBLIC,
A DICTATORSHIP,
AND A CIVIL WAR

If the history of Afghanistan has been marked in the past by fighting and conflict, modern times have not been any kinder. Factions within the nation continue to exist. Leaders have tried to obtain political and economic assistance from foreign countries without giving up Afghanistan's independence. The Soviet Union invaded Afghanistan in December 1979 in support of one faction and found its army under attack by the guerrilla fighters called *mujahideen*. The Soviet armed forces finally withdrew ten years later, leaving the various Afghan groups with new problems of working together without a common enemy.

THE REPUBLIC OF AFGHANISTAN

When a republic was proclaimed after Zahir Shah was forced out, the government was run by Daoud as a dictatorship. Jobs were given to Daoud's relatives and friends. He created a constitution in 1977, but it provided for only one political party, and

Strengthening the ties of Afghanistan with the Soviet Union, Prime Minister Mohammad Daoud (at right) flew to Moscow in 1959 at the invitation of the Soviet government. Premier Nikita Khrushchev (at left) met him at the airport.

Daoud was voted president for a six-year term.

Daoud wanted to see his country's economy grow quickly. He wanted communications improved, a railroad built, and mineral resources tapped. To do these things, he tripled taxes and sought foreign aid from both the East and the West, as well as from the Arab countries. He tried to place the total economy under state control. He nationalized the financial institutions and proposed a seven-year plan for economic development. He announced, but made little progress with, a modest plan for redistributing land.

In foreign affairs, he adopted a policy of neutrality, trying to maintain good relations with both the United States and the Soviet Union. In 1975 he renewed for ten years a Soviet-Afghan Treaty of

Supporters of the 1978 April Revolution opposing Daoud's government demonstrated in the streets of Kabul. Daoud and his family were killed in this successful military coup.

Neutrality and Non-Aggression. Because he brought up the Pushtunistan issue, his relationship with Pakistan deteriorated and required some involvement by the Soviets and Iran to smooth things out.

Political opponents attacked Daoud with increasing frequency. In 1978 he arrested seven leaders of the People's Democratic Party of Afghanistan (PDPA). He also began a purge of the army and government officials to weed out those not loyal to him. On April 27, 1978, the commanders of his military and air force successfully carried out a coup, taking over the government. This action became known as the Great *Saur*, or "April," Revolution. The PDPA leaders who had been imprisoned were released and put in power. They abolished the 1977 constitution and renamed the country the Democratic Republic of Afghanistan (DRA).

TARAKI AND AMIN REGIMES

The new government centered power in a Revolutionary Council. The PDPA became the only authorized political party. Nur Mohammad Taraki was the president of the Revolutionary Council and prime minister.

Since the PDPA had announced no program for reform, their five-year plan was not published until August, 1979. The plan proposed a state socialist system. Economic growth was targeted at 5 percent each year. Universal primary education was to be in place by 1984, and a major adult literacy program was announced. Land reform was to reduce rural indebtedness. Land was to be distributed to persons who had none. The tradition of dowries in order for marriages to take place was to be abolished.

The leaders hoped to gain the support of the masses and to destroy the political power of the landowners. The party had the backing of some of the intellectual and professional groups. However, the call for land reform and an adult literacy program created great opposition. Almost all the provinces experienced revolts, and thousands of people flooded into Pakistan and Iran. The country's economy was hurt seriously.

In September 1979, Taraki was overthrown by Hafizullah Amin, who had been a major officeholder in the regime. Now he assumed the presidency of the Revolutionary Council. Taraki was murdered the next month.

If anything, Amin was even more radical in putting down

Hafizullah Amin held a press conference a few days after he took power, hoping to gain some support for his regime.

opposition with even stronger campaigns against the rebels in the provinces. To try to get support, he appointed a committee to draft a new constitution and established a new organization, the National Organization for the Defense of the Revolution in the DRA.

Amin did not succeed in winning over or putting down the rebels. More people left Afghanistan, becoming refugees. Amin accused the United States and a raft of other countries of helping the rebels. In 1979, the United States ambassador, Adolph Dubs, was killed when he was kidnapped, and the Americans cut their aid.

Amin turned to the Soviet Union for military and economic support. However, he was not happy with the Soviets, who urged that he take a more moderate position in order to gain broader backing within the country. Finally, in December 1979, Soviet forces invaded Afghanistan and overthrew Amin, who was later executed.

THE KARMAL REGIME

Babrak Karmal was installed as the new leader. He faced a divided party, a weak economy, and an ineffective government

Famine and war drove millions of Afghans across the border into Pakistan during the 1980s. These refugees lined up to receive a supply of milk in a camp near Peshawar.

and army. The army, which had numbered ninety thousand in 1978, was down two-thirds in 1981 because of desertions. Karmal tried to depend on other services, such as police and revolutionary guards, but he had to rely on the Soviet army.

Karmal tried to modify parts of the land and social reform programs in order to get more support. In 1985 he called for a meeting of a Loya Jirgah, followed by a meeting of the tribes in September.

However, famine resulted from the civil war and dislocations of population caused people to move from the countryside into Kabul. Refugees fled to neighboring countries. It is estimated that about 3.2 million fled to Pakistan and 2.1 million to Iran. Mujahideen carried out guerrilla actions against the government,

Mujahideen used modern weaponry in primitive conditions while fighting the government and its Soviet ally. These "holy warriors" are carrying ordnance, or large shells, along a mountain path (left) and preparing to launch a U.S.-made Stinger ground-to-air missile (right).

damaging roads and communications, and taking over the government in many parts of the country.

Mujahideen were split into many different groups representing local loyalties. Often they operated from bases in the refugee camps in Pakistan and Iran. At first they were not well armed, but by 1984 they received outside support from such nations as the United States and the People's Republic of China. Mujahideen especially appreciated the U.S. Stinger ground-to-air missiles. In 1985, seven of the major Sunni groups based in the Peshawar region formed an alliance called the *Ittehad-i-Islami-Afghan Mujahideen,* or "Islamic Union of Afghan Mujahideen" (IUAM). In 1987 an eight-group alliance brought together Shiite Afghan groups based in Iran as the Islamic Coalition Council of Afghanistan (ICCA).

Karmal government officials tried to control the country and to attack the guerrillas. They bombed villages suspected of harboring mujahideen. They tried sealing off the Pakistan border. Shelling and raids across the border became common.

Mohammad Najibullah (at right) welcomed the commanders of his units to a meeting in 1988.

The government also attempted to broaden its support base by including nonparty people in office. In a vote for local offices, it was claimed that 60 percent of those elected were not members of the official party. Representatives of the tribes and nationalities were made members of the Council of Ministries. A commission was set up to draft a new constitution.

THE NAJIBULLAH REGIME
AND NATIONAL RECONCILIATION

On May 4, 1986, the former head of the secret service, Dr. Mohammad Najibullah, was appointed head of the government in place of Karmal. Najibullah pressed for compromise and unity. The Central Committee of the PDPA instituted a unilateral cease-fire for six months beginning in January 1987. Land reform was practically dropped. Other political parties were tolerated under certain conditions.

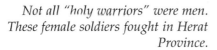
Not all "holy warriors" were men. These female soldiers fought in Herat Province.

Najibullah got rid of the remaining backers of Karmal on the Central Committee. He called for a session of the Loya Jirgah that unanimously elected Najibullah president of the country and ratified a new constitution. This constitution provided for more than one political party, adopted a two-house legislature, gave great powers to the president, who had a seven-year term of office, and changed the nation's name from the Democratic Republic to the Republic of Afghanistan. In 1988 elections for the legislature were held.

Mujahideen were having none of these changes. They boycotted the elections and set up their own resistance government. The IUAM in 1988 announced a twenty-eight-member interim coalition government with half the seats held by their members and the remainder by representatives of the refugees and "good Muslims" from Kabul. Ahmad Shah was named president and prime minister. The IUAM also came up with a proposed constitution based on Islamic ideas for an Islamic State of Afghanistan. The IUAM proposal was opposed by both the regular Kabul government and the Iran-based ICCA. The latter objected that the government included no representatives from non-IUAM mujahideen groups.

THE ROLE OF THE SOVIET UNION

The Soviets justified their 1979 invasion on the basis of their 1978 Treaty of Friendship and Good Neighborliness signed with Daoud. They claimed that Amin, who was plotting to divide up his country with foreign powers, had been overthrown by an Afghan revolution. It was the new government that had requested Soviet help. However, the Soviet newspaper, *Red Star,* reported in 1992 after the change in governments there, that back in 1979 the Soviet leader, Leonid Brezhnev, had decided to send troops to Afghanistan at least two weeks before the Afghan invitation.

Other nations did not buy the official explanation of Soviet involvement in Afghanistan. The United Nations General Assembly, the Organization of the Islamic Conference, the Association of South East Asian Nations, and the Non-Aligned Movement—all demanded Soviet withdrawal of troops. Pakistan and Western nations also opposed the Soviet action. Negotiations begun under United Nations auspices in Geneva, Switzerland, in 1981 continued to 1988.

The presence of Soviet troops in Afghanistan became increasingly unpopular with the Soviet people. More than fourteen thousand Soviet soldiers died in the ten-year operation. In 1986 the Soviet Union made a token withdrawal of six regiments of between six thousand and eight thousand men.

The Geneva negotiations produced five documents: (1) an agreement between Pakistan and Afghanistan regarding noninterference in each other's internal affairs, (2) international guarantees of Afghan independence, (3) arrangements for voluntary and free return of some five million refugees from Pakistan and Iran, (4) a

When the Soviet Union withdrew its army from Afghanistan in 1989, those soldiers looked as happy to be going home as the Afghanis were to see them leave.

timetable for further withdrawal of Soviet troops, and (5) establishment of a fifty-person United Nations monitoring force. The Soviet troops were to leave by 1989.

These agreements were reached without mujahideen or Iran taking part directly. Moreover, agreement was not reached on many issues that might have brought greater stability. Both mujahideen and the Soviet-backed government forces continued to receive arms and to fight.

The Soviet ambassador met with the IUAM, but negotiations broke down over the demand of the IUAM that no members of Najibullah's government should serve in any future government. The Soviets insisted on a role for the PDPA officials. Nevertheless, the Soviets, under pressure from their own people, withdrew all their troops from Afghanistan by February 1989.

The Soviets claimed that they had 100,000 troops in Afghanistan, but the West estimated the number to be closer to 115,000. They fought a high-tech war with only limited support by the Afghan army. On the other hand, mujahideen, who numbered about 100,000, fought a primitive war with emphasis on guerrilla tactics. Yet mujahideen were the first group of fighters to drive out a Russian army since Peter the Great, tsar of Russia, began the southward expansion of his empire three hundred years earlier.

THE CIVIL WAR

With the Soviet withdrawal, many expected the Najibullah regime to collapse. Instead, it proved resilient. While mujahideen attacked, they were hampered by lack of tactics other than the guerrilla warfare at which they had been so successful.

Also, mujahideen were made up of many factions—some fundamentalist Islamic groups and others more moderate in the reforms they wanted. These groups had to work together and carve out their power positions with respect to each other.

Both mujahideen and the Najibullah governments were supplied with arms by their friends. The Afghan air force and the fifteen hundred Scud missiles left in the hands of the government were used against the mujahideen. In 1990 an army officer tried to overthrow the government. Planes from the Afghan air force strafed Kabul government offices. The coup attempt failed.

Not until April 1992 was Najibullah forced out and mujahideen moved into Kabul. In the fourteen years of war, one million people had died. More than five million—about one-third of the remaining population—had fled the country and become refugees.

Prayer is important to the Afghans. The Islamic warriors on both sides halted a battle to pray, as required by their faith.

Nearly 100,000 acres (40,469 hectares) of forest were destroyed during the war. An estimated 500,000 farm animals were killed. To make matters worse, ten million land mines are still scattered around the country, creating continuing hazards for all.

MUJAHIDEEN IN POWER

In April 1992, mujahideen took Kabul. Most of the coalition fighters were led by Commander Ahmed Shah Masoud, but another rebel leader, Gulbuddin Hekmatyar, headed other troops. Masoud is a Tajik and Hekmatyar, a Pushtun. Hekmatyar wanted

Two Afghan leaders after the Soviets withdrew were Ahmed Shah Masoud (left) and Sibghatullah Mojadedi (right).This picture of Masoud was often displayed on tanks driven by his soldiers.

strict application of Islamic law, while Masoud favored a more moderate approach.

The coalition had arranged for Sibghatullah Mojadedi, who had been a professor of Islamic philosophy at Kabul University, to be the interim president. Later, he was to turn over the presidency to Burhanuddin Rabbani, the political leader of the *Jamiat-i-Islami,* or "Society of Islam Party." Masoud was the military leader of that party. However, Hekmatyar refused to participate because of the dominance of people who were not of the Pushtun group.

The new president, Mojadedi, announced a fifty-member interim commission to govern and prepare for democratic elections. The council was to be made up of five members from each of the ten principal factions. Amnesty was given to all members of the former government except for Najibullah, whom the Afghans wanted tried for war crimes. He remains under protection at the United Nations Mission in Kabul. Under the new government, the sale of alcohol was banned, and women were required to cover their heads and wear Islamic dress. The former National Assembly was dissolved and the Communist Party was outlawed. The former chief justice was killed.

The president appointed thirty-six cabinet members but held open eight offices, including the office of prime minister, as an inducement to Hekmatyar to join the coalition government. This did not succeed. He continued fighting against the coalition. Minorities of Shiite Muslims and Hazaras, people from the mountains of central Afghanistan, were given cabinet posts. While Iran wanted the two million plus Afghan refugees within its borders to return to their own country, those refugees, who were mostly Shiites, feared persecution as a minority.

Rabbani took over as president and was reelected in December by the religious and tribal leaders. Early in 1993, troubles in Tajikistan, a former republic in the Soviet Union, caused some 120,000 refugees to flee across the border into Afghanistan—some swimming the Amu Darya River to escape. The Tajik rebels then fought with Russian and Tajik forces along the Afghan border. The Afghan government denied any involvement. However, in December 1993, Russia and Turkmenistan signed an agreement providing for Russian troops to be stationed along the border with Afghanistan and Iran.

The $10-million aid package that the United Nations announced in 1992 for food and medicine did little to change Afghanistan's bleak economic picture. The currency exchange rate has dropped as much as 300 percent. With the continued fighting, none of the international aid donors can feel it is worthwhile to give money to build something that will only be destroyed in the

President Burhanuddin Rabbani, seen here leading prayers, was the leader of the Society of Islam Party.

next bombing raid. In April 1994, the United Nations appealed for $62 million to support its programs in Afghanistan for a six-month period. However, only $6 million was collected, in contrast to $35 million for the previous six-month period.

Then on January 1, 1994, the militia of General Abdul Rashid Dostam in alliance with Hekmatyar launched an attack to oust Rabbani. Dostam is the same Uzbek leader who, as a general in the Communist army in 1992, defected to a coalition of the mujahideen, thereby helping to overthrow the Soviet-backed government. Dostam did not sign the peace agreement with the other military factions.

The government counterattacked with heavy fighting in Mazar-i Sharif in the north where Dostam had his headquarters. However, Dostam drove the forces back and maintained control of the airstrip from which he was able to launch a bombing attack against Kabul that set fire to the presidential palace.

In June the government forces were able to drive the rebels

The Afghan Army on parade in Jalalabad

from their bases in the northern, southern, and eastern sections of
Kabul. They captured a thousand-member force loyal to Dostam.
The rebels launched a bombing attack on government forces in
Herat, and the government responded with a bombing of rebel
forces on the eastern fringes of Kabul. Between January and June
of 1994, as many as 2,500 were killed.

On June 28, 1994, the Supreme Court ordered a six-month
extension of Rabbani's presidential term that technically expired
on that date. Also during the summer, a new group sprang up
among the Pushtun people. Called the Taliban, this Islamic fundamentalist militia had the aim of establishing peace and ultimately
an Islamic state. The group gathered strength and had military
victories against the forces of Hekmatyar. They are reported to

*Taliban soldiers fighting against Afghan government troops in 1995.
Such fighting destroyed most of Kabul, the capital city.*

have gained control of ten of Afghanistan's provinces, 40 percent
of the land area almost exclusively in Pushtun territory, and 20,000
forces, 200 tanks, and a dozen fighter jets.

The Afghan Defense Minister, Commander Masoud, gave the
group political and military support since they were fighting
Hekmatyar who was besieging Kabul. However, Masoud now has
pushed the Taliban back from Kabul.

In February 1995, the United Nations was trying to negotiate
the transfer of power from Rabbani to a broad-based council that
was to be an interim group leading to the formation of a perma-
nent government. The Taliban were not party to the agreement,
but they promised not to interfere with the plans so long as
Rabbani, Hekmatyar, and former Communists were barred from
power and a true Islamic state ultimately resulted. Rabbani
declined to cede power to the council unless the Taliban reversed
their decision not to join the council. The Taliban, considering the

council corrupt and unreliable, refused.

It can only be hoped that Afghanistan can regain some stability so that the country can recover from the fighting that has gone on for so many years. Many outsiders are concerned that an entire generation of Afghans with no trade other than fighting will have difficulty adjusting to peace conditions in their own country and may stir up rebellions in the newly independent countries adjoining Afghanistan.

Generations of Afghan children have experienced only war or, like these children, the sadness of being refugees from their own land.

Chapter 6

AFGHAN LIFE

The history of Afghanistan provides good evidence that there are many variations on the basic structure of Afghan life. Group loyalties are stronger than national Afghan identity unless there is a foreign threat.

GOVERNMENT

Since Amanullah's reign, Afghanistan has had many constitutions. In addition to providing that Islam shall be the state religion and that Pushtu and Dari are to be the official languages, the constitutions have established basic governmental structures.

The Loya Jirgah is the highest governmental body, consisting of executive, legislative, and judicial leaders, representatives of the provinces elected by the people, and at least fifty prominent leaders appointed by the president. This group elects the president, declares war or accepts an armistice, and decides all major questions regarding the country's destiny.

Afghanistan has had presidents, vice-presidents, prime

Left: Such Islamic houses of worship as this Friday Mosque at Herat play a vital role in the lives of most Afghans.

This Loya Jirgah, *or grand assembly, that met in 1989 included 650 representatives from various factions in Afghanistan. Some of the representatives were women.*

ministers, a council of ministers, a constitutional council, a judicial system, and a two-house legislature called the *Meli Shura*. Local government occurs in the provinces, districts, cities, and wards.

RELIGION

Islam is the state religion for the country. All Muslims follow the prophet Muhammad, who lived in what is now Saudi Arabia in the sixth and seventh centuries. However, there are two major groups—the Sunnis and the Shiites. This division has existed since soon after Muhammad's death and has led to customs that are different because the people follow different interpretations of Islamic law and different methods of selecting leadership. With 80 percent of the population of Afghanistan Sunni, the Shiites are in the minority. (There are also small minority groups of Hindus, Sikhs, and Jews.)

Revelations from God to Muhammad were compiled in the *Qur'an*, or Koran, the holy book of the Muslims. The five duties of

Religion is the focus of life in Afghanistan.
Above: prayers being said in a Shiite mosque;
right: a center, or school, where men
study the Qur'an

Muslims have been called the "Five Pillars of Islam." They are: (1) to believe and say the creed: "There is no god but God (Allah), and Muhammad is his Prophet,"(2) to pray five times daily, (3) to give to the poor, (4) to fast during the month of Ramadan, and (5) to make a pilgrimage to Muhammad's birthplace in Mecca (in present-day Saudi Arabia) if the money is available to do so.

The building where Muslims gather for prayers and to hear a message is called a mosque. Muslims believe that to portray a human being is to make an idol, which is forbidden. Therefore, Islamic art has developed an eye for abstract design. Many mosques are decorated with beautiful tiles. Because passages from the Qur'an are often portrayed, the writing style, the calligraphy, can be very beautiful.

Religion permeates the daily life of the Afghans. In the matters of women's dress and the wearing of the veil, leaders have had different interpretations of what Islam permits, but they have not ignored the teachings of the faith.

Left: A Tajik bride is dressed for her wedding in traditional dress. Above: Mujahideen bury a man killed in battle in Kabul, according to Islamic rites.

Traditionally, a Muslim husband could have four wives if he could treat them the same, and he could easily divorce a wife. In many Muslim countries, secular laws have provided safeguards for women in family and property matters. Afghan women, in order to justify their activity in social and educational programs, cite the verses of the Qur'an that praise women.

While religion was a powerful force uniting mujahideen against the "godless" Soviet influence, now the different interpretations of Islamic teaching are one of the problems splitting them apart.

EDUCATION

Traditional education was conducted by religious leaders in mosque schools. While these schools are still active, a modern educational system was developed as early as 1904. Children

A school in Kabul holds classes in a war-damaged building.

between the ages of ten and fourteen who had no opportunity to attend school were given special classes to cover primary education in two years. Elementary school beginning at age seven and lasting for eight years has become compulsory. Secondary education begins at age fifteen and lasts four years. In 1988 the government claimed that more than 857,000 students were in 1,348 schools. However, with the fighting throughout the country since then, many young people have been unable to attend school.

The country has one of the highest adult illiteracy rates in Asia. The government claimed to have more than twenty thousand literacy courses attended by 400,000 students in 1987. However, in 1990 a United Nations organization estimated the rate of illiteracy at 70.6 percent (males 55.9 percent and females 86.1 percent).

Higher education has been emphasized with teacher training and vocational and industrial colleges. The University of Kabul was established in 1932 with the founding of a medical school. That university has expanded and several others established at Herat, Mazar-i Sharif, and Qandahar.

Detail on this waistcoat shows the creative abilities of a Pushtun tailor.

THE ARTS

Spoken poetry has been the major literary form in Afghanistan. Memorization and recitation of verses has preserved the works of many poets from the past. One way that the Afghans pass on their tribal history is by having a talented person recite the entire family relationship of the clan with stories of historic events in which the clan had participated.

Music and dance are important to the Afghans. Their traditional instruments include drums, a stringed gourd, and a wind instrument. War dances, such as the *attan,* are performed by men. Sometimes twenty to one hundred men will dance around a stake or fire. They swing swords or guns in their right hands. Although the dance starts slowly, the pace quickens. Dancers and the musicians playing drum and flute join in traditional songs.

Afghans are famous for their leather goods, and gold and silver jewelry. They are also skilled in woodworking, making pottery, and molding tiles. Coppersmiths turn out practical items, such as pots and pans, but also works of art with intricate designs.

Afghan carpets and rugs are world famous. The wools and dyes may be prepared in the local communities. Some of the best are from Dalatabad in the northwest and from Herat. The famed Herat carpets of the sixteenth and seventeenth centuries have a red field with borders of green accented with yellow.

The arts in Afghanistan are primarily those traditional to Islam and the home. Clockwise starting above: Qur'anic singers in a mosque; an Islamic inscription done in mosaic tiles in a mosque; a primitive traditional stringed instrument; a "war dance" performed by men in the open air; and young girls demonstrating their carpet-weaving talents.

A bazaar in Kabul draws customers dressed in both traditional and modern fashion. The traditional dress of men requires that they never wear shorts or short-sleeved shirts.

Often children are involved in rug-making because their fingers are nimble and can tie the many knots required. However, if this close work is not done in good light with frequent rest breaks, it can be very hard and tiring.

SHOPPING AND BAZAARS

In peaceful times, one of the great pastimes is shopping in the bazaars to which people would bring their food and crafted items for sale. The buyers enjoy searching for items they need and picking up the news of the day at the same time.

In war conditions, shopping involves risks. In Kabul, in order to buy staples such as rice, flour, and fuel, residents have to travel to areas controlled by opposition forces. They may be stopped by soldiers suspicious that they are carrying supplies to the enemy. Then they must make the return journey to their homes with the

This medical clinic for mothers and children is run by funds from the United Nations.

same risks. Food blockades were used to starve the people in the once-prosperous capital city.

HEALTH

Drought and war have been enemies to improving the health care in Afghanistan. As of 1995, life expectancy was 42 years for males and 43 years for females—the lowest life-expectancy rate in Asia. Afghanistan also has the highest infant-mortality rate.

While the government has tried to increase the number of clinics, war conditions have complicated the work. Moreover, mujahideen, as rebels, were not able to tap these resources during the civil war. Many children were killed or maimed by land mines and rockets. Malnutrition, malaria, measles, and tuberculosis are problems. In 1993 the country suffered a cholera epidemic. Unclean water accounts for intestinal diseases.

Left: A kebab maker in a public market puts meat and vegetables on a skewer.
Right: A Tajik woman prepares a rice dish called pilaf.

FOOD

Those Afghans who can afford to will have both rice and wheat at meals, using their *nan,* or bread, as an eating tool. Most Afghans, like all the people in that part of the world, eat with the fingers of their right hand.

Rice mixed with meat and vegetables is such a common dish that the word *pilaf,* a dish made of seasoned rice, has come to mean food in general. Fast-cooking rice, or "minute" rice, now used in the United States, was introduced by an Afghan. The nomads precooked their rice before long journeys to cut down on cooking time. *Kebabs* are meat and vegetables that are placed on a skewer and grilled over fire. The nan is usually made of whole wheat flour and baked in ovens built into the ground or fried on

Men often gather at teahouses, which are meant for men only. This one is in Bamian. In the cities, women have their own walled purdah parks.

griddles. Fresh fruit is plentiful. A sweet desert is *jelabi,* fried bread coated with syrup and molasses. Black or green tea may be served with the meal. A sugar lump may be soaked with tea.

Still, there are many local variations. For example, in Nuristan, rice is not common, but a kind of fondue, cheese melted with butter, is soaked up with bread.

CLOTHING AND WOMEN

While Western dress was adopted by many in the cities during the time of King Zahir Shah through the Najibullah regime, a return to more traditional clothing may be in the offing with the mujahideen in power. Both men and women traditionally wear long cotton shirts and baggy trousers. The men often wear turbans that can indicate their tribal affiliation by the way they are tied. In the cold weather, heavy coats are a necessity.

Women also wear a dress with long skirts, often in bright colors, over their trousers. They quite often wear shawls. A fundamentalist woman must wear a *chaderi,* a long covering that reveals only her eyes, when she leaves her home.

Family ties are very important to Afghans. Thus marriages,

Left: Even in a religion class for women only, many women keep their heads covered.
Right: Wrestling is one of the most popular Olympic sports.

births, and deaths receive due celebration. Traditionally, Afghans have been very protective of their women. It has been only recently that the leaders have encouraged women to appear in public and to leave off the veil. These new patterns took hold in cities like Kabul more readily than in the countryside villages.

Now the women of the cities fear the extent to which mujahideen will force them to return to the old ways. While some, like a woman who is a television news commentator, have no problem in adopting the head covering if it means that they continue to work, others fear that the dress code is the first step to confining women to their homes again. Some complain that after thirty years of freedom, they are being forced back into the Middle Ages. Still, because about 75 percent of the teachers are women, the government will probably not be able to ban them from public jobs.

The national game of buzkashi calls for great horsemanship.
Afghans are fierce competitors at sports.

RECREATION

While some Afghans like soccer, field hockey, and golf, they
have done best in Olympic events in the wrestling and weight-
lifting competitions. The latter are closer to the traditional Afghan
sports.

One famous traditional sport, *buzkashi,* requires skill and horsemanship. Riders try to carry the headless carcass of a calf or goat
over a goal. This sport is played both in stadiums and out in the
countryside, where it originated.

Children's games include tag, blind-man's bluff, kite-flying,
and hopscotch. Parents may make dolls for girls and slingshots
for the boys. Pigeon-raising in the cities also turns into a challenge
to capture someone else's birds. Winter snow provides plenty of
opportunity for snowball fights.

Bamitan Valley is a fertile valley in the central highlands.

Chapter 7

THE ECONOMY

To measure the Afghan economy in terms of numbers has always been difficult. Communication between the countryside and the capital, Kabul, has never been good. The rugged terrain of Afghanistan and the suspicions that exist between city dwellers and those who live on the land have meant that government officials must often guess at the statistics they report.

Added to this traditional problem of communications is the fighting that has been going on since 1979. The people turning out government reports may not have access to parts of the country that are under the control of the other side. Counting up numbers may not be as important as getting supplies where they are needed.

The movement of populations within the country and across its borders upset the economy. The droughts in the early 1970s reduced the normal production of food that usually is enough to supply the country's needs. Then, just as outside aid was helping the nation get back to normal, the Soviet invasion upset projects that had been in the planning stage.

ECONOMIC PLANNING

While Afghanistan was a busy trading nation during the days of the land caravan routes from East to West, the advent of sea routes in the fifteenth century diverted this trade. Silks and spices

Sheep wool is one of the important agricultural products of Afghanistan.

were carried in ships instead of across land, and Afghanistan had no ocean ports. Even centuries later, when railways were being built elsewhere, the Afghanistan mountains and politics did not make routes through the country possible.

Modern economic development in Afghanistan did not begin until the 1930s when the National Bank was established. Before then, there were only a few workshops in Kabul that supplied the army and one small hydroelectric plant. With the formation of the bank, private companies were created. While some of these companies were in the textile and sugar businesses, most traded in the skins and wool of a breed of sheep called karakul. The skin from the young lambs is sold as Persian lamb.

ONE MAN'S STORY

The beginning of this free enterprise era is reflected in the life of Abdul Aziz Londoni. Londoni's father had an import-export business in which he sold fox furs and embroidered Afghan sheep-

Cotton was one of the products supplied to the Soviet Union by Londoni during the early years of Afghanistan's world trade.

skin coats in India in exchange for tea, spices, and cotton cloth that he sold in the Afghan bazaars. When that business almost collapsed during World War I, Londoni sold all his furniture and household goods and bought Afghan carpets. These carpets he traded for karakul skins in Tashkent and Bukhara across the border in Soviet central Asia. At this point, most of the other merchants thought he was crazy.

However, he sold the skins in Peshawar for a huge profit. He invested that profit in tea, which he shipped and sold in Afghanistan. Thus began the karakul industry that was to bring much foreign currency to the nation.

Londoni went to England in 1922 and introduced his karakul skins there. Until World War II, England bought almost all of the karakul skins that Afghanistan could supply. Abdul Aziz acquired the tag "Londoni" for this marketing skill exhibited in London, England.

Londoni returned to his country through Moscow and discovered that the Soviets wanted cotton. He figured that cotton could be grown in Afghanistan, so he made a deal to supply raw cotton for payment in gold and cotton cloth. The Soviets began to

Kunduz province, where this village is located, is a major source of cotton.

compete with him in the markets for karakul, so Londoni transferred most of his money into cotton.

In Moscow, Londoni met a fellow Afghan, Zabuli, who was selling wool to Russia. The two men formed a partnership. Zabuli started the bank that became the investment bank that backed most of the capital development in Afghanistan before World War II.

Zabuli and Londoni opened up new lands for growing cotton and expanded operations to include oilseed, soap, and ceramics, as well as the ginning and pressing of raw cotton. Londoni built houses and a hospital for his workers. He opened up the Kunduz and Pul-i-Khumri areas for cotton production. Settlers had to drain the malarial swamps. The governor of the area at that time could have hurt Londoni's efforts, but instead he backed them with all the resources he had, including forced labor.

The work of Londoni, Zabuli, and the governor continued until 1953 when Daoud became prime minister. Then the Kunduz Cotton Company and other free enterprise efforts came under the

*The modern plaza in front of the Blue Mosque in Masar-e Sharif is
one of many structures improved under recent government plans.*

supervision of a government that wanted to emphasize public
rather than private development.

GOVERNMENT PLANS

Daoud needed foreign money to back his five-year plan of
economic development. When the United States would agree only
to aid specific projects, Daoud turned to the Soviets. By playing
the superpowers against each other in the Cold War, he won some
$900 million from the Soviet Union, while the United States offered

Transportation in Afghanistan is more likely to be this donkey cart on the road into Herat (left) than the modern buses found in Kabul (right).

about $500 million, the second-largest amount of foreign aid.

Daoud's first five-year plan emphasized building roads and airports, plus establishing thirty-two industrial projects. However, the results did not match his dreams. His second five-year plan was to undertake government development of power, gas, cement, and chemical industries. The government had problems in finding operators and managers to run the plants. The next effort centered on finding projects that would yield results more quickly. These goals also proved difficult to achieve even though he overthrew King Zahir in 1973 and took total control of the government.

Many of the projects that Daoud planned were not accomplished, but he achieved much in the years before his own overthrow in 1978. The government built 1,727 miles (2,780 kilometers) of paved roads, two international and twenty-nine local airports, and many dams and bridges. Motor vehicle registrations went from sixteen thousand in 1962 to fifty-two thousand in 1971.

Afghans fleeing war in Jalalabad could take only what they could carry.

Cotton cloth production quadrupled, and soap, sugar, and coal industry production rose between 100 and 300 percent. Cement and shoe manufacturing began. Electrical production increased 900 percent. Natural gas production was started, providing an export to the Soviet Union. Industrial employment rose from eighteen thousand in 1962 to twenty-seven thousand in 1971. More than sixty private industries were established, employing nearly five thousand people.

SOVIET INFLUENCE

With Soviet troops in Afghanistan, Western aid to the government stopped. With guerrilla fighting, farming was disrupted. With shortages increasing, the Soviets used food as a way of rewarding people loyal to them. The threat of starvation and fighting forced people to move into the cities. Afghan refugees who fled the country caused further disruptions in production. By

Wheat and similar crops can be grown only in fertile valleys where water accumulates during the rainy season (left). Opium poppies (right) are a more profitable crop, often grown on infertile land useless for other crops.

1982, the nation depended on the Soviet Union for 84 percent of its machinery, 65 percent of its cotton fabrics, 96 percent of its petroleum products, and all its sugar. Nonmilitary aid from the Soviet Union rose from $34 million in 1979 to $284 million in 1981. By 1984 the Soviets had spend $12 billion, most of which the Afghans were supposed to repay. By 1987, the Soviet Union was underwriting 40 percent of the civilian budget. With the Soviet withdrawal of troops and the Soviet's own financial worries, the Afghan situation was bleak.

Although United Nations aid has been pledged, mujahideen face problems of rebuilding the country and finding ways to handle the return of refugees. Until Afghanistan has political stability, it will be difficult to attract foreign money for this effort.

AGRICULTURE

Agriculture is the most important factor in the economy. Of course, much of the land is too rugged to be used for agriculture. However, only about half of the land that is possible to use is cultivated. A small area of the irrigated land produces most of the crops. Irrigation, often elaborate, is essential in a place that is subject to droughts.

Many children throughout Afghanistan work in the poppy fields. The round capsules on the plants produce a milky substance that oozes out when they are cut. Heroin and other drugs are derived from the fluid.

Wheat is the principal crop. When wheat production drops, livestock has to be killed. Afghanistan is capable of growing wheat, seed cotton, rice, maize (corn), barley, fruit, sugar beets, and sugarcane in substantial amounts.

Opium poppies are a crop that is illegal but very profitable because poppies are the source of the drugs opium and heroin. Grown in the provinces of Nangarhar, Badakhshan, Helmand, and Pakita, the poppies are refined in laboratories in Nangarhar Province and across the border in Pakistan. The heroin produced by refining opium is then exported to India and Iran and on to the United States and Europe. Hashish, which, like marijuana, comes from the hemp plant, is another export. Because of Afghanistan's

Water is one of the most precious resources in Afghanistan. This sheltered water house in Herat is used by both residents and ducks.

failure to control these shipments, the United States has been reluctant to send in aid.

Forests have been shrinking, and with the fighting going on, conservation was not a priority. However, evergreen trees supply wood for construction, oaks for fuel, pistachio trees for nuts, and gum trees for resin.

INDUSTRY, MINING, AND ENERGY

Handicrafts, such as carpet-making and weaving, contribute more to the economy than modern industry. Cotton is the largest and oldest industry. Cement production was encouraged by the Soviets with Czechs providing help in the building of a factory. While attempts were made to encourage private enterprise, even in 1986 and 1987, the private sector amounted to only 11.8 percent of the total industrial income.

Afghanistan is rich in coal, salt, chromium, iron ore, silver, gold, fluorite, talc, mica, copper, and lapis lazuli. The problem is how to get to where these resources are found and how to get them out to a market. Only when these problems can be solved is it commercially worthwhile to mine these minerals.

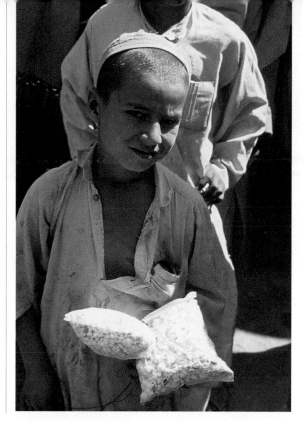

This Afghan refugee child, who would rather sell popcorn than beg, has learned sad but valuable lessons in both survival and contributing to the economy.

Natural gas was Afghanistan's major export. In 1988 and 1989, more than 90 percent of the natural gas was piped to the Soviet Union to pay for imports and debts. The pipelines were sometimes blown up by mujahideen. Existing fields may be used up by the end of the twentieth century.

Hard coal, centered at Pul-e-Khumri, is mined with equipment supplied by Czechoslovakia. Iron ore has been discovered at Hajigak in Bamian Province, but it is at a high elevation. Copper mining and smelting at Ainak near Kabul look promising. The Soviets began to mine uranium from newly discovered fields.

Two small oil fields in the northern part of the country may help in the future to balance the imports of oil products from foreign sources such as Iran and Russia. Hydroelectric and thermal power stations supply about 80 percent of the energy used. A steel smelter was started at the Jangalak factory area.

LABOR

In the countryside, the pattern of Afghan life has remained very traditional. A son is expected to follow his father's work.

Cloth is an important Afghan product, with large quantities used by women for their chaderi and men for their turbans.

Almost as soon as he can walk and talk, he is expected to look after the sheep and other animals of the family. Girls are expected to contribute to the care of the family. They are even less likely than the boys to be sent to school.

In the city, there are other opportunities. However, the intellectual and professional class always has been small, even for women with education. Only a small number of women are in the workforce, primarily as teachers.

Unemployment, because of the damage to the industrial and agricultural systems and because of the return of refugees, will provide problems for the new regime. However, where tribal allegiance is strong, the practice of caring for others in the family provides a home-grown system of social services. The war has disrupted this system.

The Cold War is over, but the former superpowers have economic problems of their own. Afghanistan needs to find ways of rebuilding from the destruction of the fighting and ways to unite the Afghans to plan for the future.

Among the greatest resources Afghanistan has are its fascinating scenery and history. These attractions could bring in tourists to augment the nation's economy. However, in order to attract tourists, the nation must first develop stability, good airline service, and adequate tourist facilities.

Above: Carpet sellers in Kabul sell their beautiful rugs at open bazaars.
Below: The capital of Afghanistan since 1775 is Kabul, seen here in 1973 before much of the city was damaged by wars.

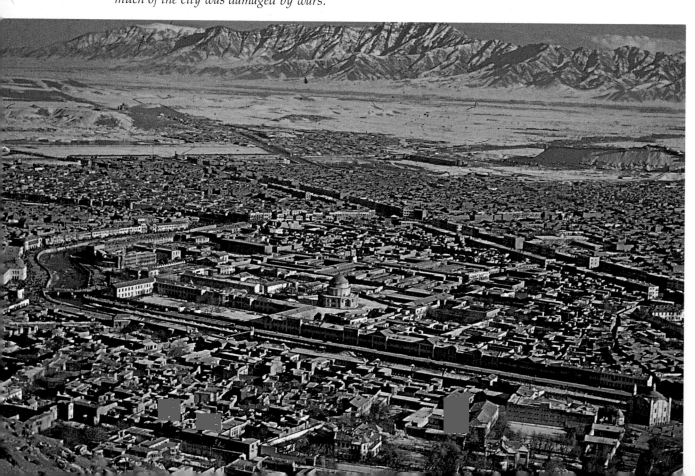

Chapter 8

PEOPLE AND PLACES

"Variety" is the one word that best describes the people and the landscape of Afghanistan. The people come from different ethnic backgrounds. They speak different languages. Some reside in the cities. Some have settled in small villages and raise crops. Some are nomads who keep on the move herding animals over large areas.

ETHNIC GROUPS

The Pushtuns live primarily in the southern and eastern parts, but they also have some members in the west and north. Some of the Pushtun tribes have settled down while others are still nomadic. Large numbers of Pushtuns live in neighboring Pakistan. Two of the largest groups of Pushtuns are the Durranis and the Ghilzais who live around the cities of Qandahar, Ghazni, and Kabul. They usually are strict Sunni Muslims and speak Pushto.

The Tajiks live in the Kabul and Badakhshan areas of the northeast and in the Herat region, though there are settlements elsewhere, too. The Tajiks have been mostly farmers and artisans, and they are not divided into well-defined tribal groups. Mainly Sunni Muslims, they speak Dari.

The Nuristanis live in the eastern part of the country and were

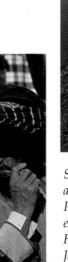

Some people of Afghanistan (clockwise from top left): a nomad boy from the desert mountains of Bamian; Pushtun people and their cattle; companionable readers in a Tajik village; Turkmen tribesmen of the Hindu Kush; Nuristani soldiers on parade in Jalalabad; Uzbek men at a market in Mazar-i Sharif.

forcibly converted to Sunni Islam in the late nineteenth century. They speak Kafiri dialects.

The Hazaras traditionally came from the central mountain area of Hazarajat. However, because of an expanding population, they have moved to the cities, especially Kabul. They speak Dari and most are Shiite Muslims.

Several groups show a Turkic or Mongolian origin in their appearance and in the style of their houses. Among these are the Chahar Aimaks, located mostly in the western part of the central mountain region. The Uzbeks (mostly farmers) and the Turkmens (primarily seminomadic herdsmen) are located in the region north of the Hindu Kush and in the extreme northwest. Many of these people, along with other smaller tribes, speak Turkic and are Sunni Muslims.

Because of some intermixing of these groups, there is a wide variation in appearance. Skin, eyes, and hair color come in many combinations mixed with Caucasoid or Mongoloid features. Thus there are people with high cheekbones and Mongoloid eye features with blond hair and blue eyes. In more isolated areas, there is less intermixing.

KABUL

Kabul is the capital and largest city of Afghanistan. It serves as the cultural and economic center of the nation. The city lies on the Kabul River in the valley between the Asmai and Sherdawaza Mountains. Roads from Kabul lead to most of the Afghan provinces and beyond the borders of the country.

Kabul controls mountain passes, giving it a strategic location.

This destroyed street in Kabul was once a major boulevard.

It has been the capital off and on since the eighth century. Genghis Khan captured and almost destroyed the city. Kabul has often been the center of fighting over the years, including the recent occupation by troops of the Soviet Union and the later assaults between mujahideen factions.

As the capital, the city contains many historical monuments, such as tombs of its leaders. Since the days of Babur, the gardens of Kabul have been famous. The parliament and government offices are in the Dar ul-Aman Palace. The University of Kabul and a number of industries are located here. Most of the residents of Kabul speak Dari, although there are also many Pushtuns living in the city.

Shells, rockets, bombs, and machine guns damaged much of the city, not only during the ouster of the Soviets but also more recently in the fighting between factions of mujahideen. From January to July, 1994, a third of the city's 1.1 million people fled to safer areas. Many of those who remained had to live in conditions

Qandahar province (above) is a major agricultural region. Its heart is the city of Qandahar (right), which was the first capital of Afghanistan.

of hardship and suffering. Many of the landmarks have been damaged. The blue dome of the Haji Yaqub Mosque has been blackened by fire.

QANDAHAR

Qandahar is the capital of a province of the same name in south-central Afghanistan. It is located on a plain next to the Tarnak River. A commercial center, it lies at the junction of the roads from Kabul and Herat in Afghanistan and Quetta in

Red pompoms enliven the transportation at Herat. This city was built primarily during the reign of Ahmad Shah Durrani.

Pakistan. With irrigated farmland nearby, food processing is important to Qandahar along with textile factories. It has an international airport.

A number of cities have been built on this strategic location since the days of Alexander the Great. The Old City, as it is now known, was built by Ahmad Shah Durrani in the eighteenth century. In 1747 Qandahar became the first capital of the unified Afghanistan. Ahmad Shah Durrani's mausoleum is one of the important buildings in the city, which is populated primarily by Pushtun people. The Soviet Union converted a United States-built international airport near the city into a military base.

Found in all the cities are open bazaars, or markets, such as this one in Jalalabad.

HERAT

Herat lies in western Afghanistan on the Harirud River, south of the Safid Kuh Mountains. With good agricultural land around it, it is not surprising that it is densely populated. The city is the transportation and economic center of western Afghanistan. An airport is located near Herat.

From the days of Alexander the Great, a number of important cities have been built at this site. During the Arab conquest in A.D. 660, it was a center of the Muslim world. The Mongols destroyed much of the city. Perhaps Herat's finest period was after it was captured by Timur about 1393. Then it became one of the great centers of science and culture. Herat carpets and miniature paintings are famous.

Beautiful mosques are the focus of many cities. This ornate carving, being viewed by a woman pilgrim, is at Mazar-i Sharif.

Both Persia and Afghanistan claimed the city, but it finally became part of Afghanistan in 1863. The Soviet Union had a major military command headquarters here.

A fifteenth-century mosque and decorated minarets are among the treasures of the city. A shrine of a poet and saint, Abdullah Ansari, is still venerated by the people.

The city's history of trading is reflected in the bazaars. Light industry includes handicrafts, such as carpets, glass, and silk, textile weaving, cotton ginning, and milling of rice, flour, and oilseed. Carpets and karakul skins have been important trade items. The population is largely Tajik, Turkmen, and Uzbek.

MAZAR-I SHARIF

This city is the capital of a province in northern Afghanistan just south of the border with Uzbekistan. It is famous for the Blue Mosque, which is reputed to house the tomb of the Caliph Ali, son-in-law of Muhammad. The Shiites especially honor this shrine. A famous Islamic theology school is located at Mazar-i

The famed Blue Mosque at Mazar-i Sharif in northern Afghanistan is a "place of pilgrimage" (which is what the name means) for all Muslim faithful because it is reputed to contain the mausoleum of Muhammad's son-in-law.

Sharif. The population is largely Uzbek, Tajik, and Turkmen.

Mazar-i Sharif was included in Afghan territory in 1852. The Soviet forces had a military command in the town and began construction of a road and rail bridge across the Amu Darya, north of the city near Termez in Uzbekistan. It is a transit point for trade with neighboring countries and has an airport nearby.

The city is located in a rich agricultural district with irrigation from the Balkh River. Flour milling and the manufacture of textiles are carried on in the city.

Traffic lines up at the eastern gate of the Khyber Pass (above). The man at the left is one of the security guards at the pass.

KHYBER PASS

This important pass through the mountains connects Kabul in Afghanistan with Peshawar in Pakistan. It is rich in the history of conquerors and defenders from the fifth century B.C. when Darius I of Persia marched through it and on to the Indus River. The British era in the region has been captured in the poetry of Rudyard Kipling.

Two small rivers cut through a narrow gorge between cliffs of shale and limestone that are 600 to 1,000 feet (183 to 305 meters) high and in places no more than 600 feet (183 meters) across—a likely spot for ambush. The pass has a caravan track and a hard-surface road. A railroad on the Pakistan side passes through thirty-four tunnels and ninety-four bridges and culverts.

The Pushtun Afridi people who live in the Khyber Pass area always have been very independent and almost a law unto themselves. The pass is under the control of the Pakistan Khyber Agency.

THE FUTURE

The Afghans face the challenge of rebuilding a country that has been subject to massive devastation and extensive fighting. Whether the many groups that make up this nation can work together, only the future will tell. The education of the young people will be an important factor in providing the leadership that will be required to rebuild and develop this nation.

The military helicopter has been a symbol of the recent past in Afghanistan. Perhaps the minaret, or tower, of a mosque will be a symbol of the future.

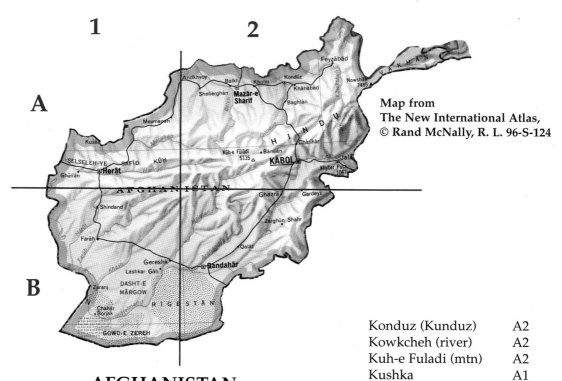

AFGHANISTAN

Occasionally the spellings of place -names used on the map are alternatives to those in the text. The differences are noted.

Andkhvoy	A2	Ghurian	A1	Konduz (Kunduz)	A2
Arghandab (river)	B2	Gowd-e Zereh	B1	Kowkcheh (river)	A2
Baghlan	A2	Harirud (river)	A1	Kuh-e Fuladi (mtn)	A2
Balkh	A2	Harut (river)	B1	Kushka	A1
Balkh (river)	A2	Helmand (river)	B1	Lashkar Fah	B1
Bamian	A2	Herat	A1	Mazar-e Sharif	
Chahar Borjak	B1	Hindu Kush	A2	(Mazar-i Sharif)	A2
Charikar	A2	Jalalabad	A2	Meymaneh	A1
Farah	B1	Kabol (Kabul)	A2	Morghab (river)	A1
Farah (river)	B1	Kabol (river)	A2	Nowshak (mtn)	A2
Feyzabad	A2	Khanabad	A2	Panj (river)	A2
Gardeyz	B2	Khash (river)	B1	Qalat	B2
Gereshk	B1	Kholm	A2	Qandahar	B2
Ghazni	B2	Khyber Pass	A2	Qonduz (Kunduz)	
				(river)	A2
				Rigestan (desert)	B1,2
				Selseleh-ye Safid Kuh	A1
				Sheberghan	A2
				Shindand	B1
				Vakhan Corridor	A2
				Zaranj	B1
				Zarghun Shahr	B2

MINI-FACTS AT A GLANCE

GENERAL INFORMATION

Official Name: Islamic State of Afghanistan.

Capital: Kabul.

Government: Constitutionally it is an Islamic state with an elected parliament. The *Loya Jirgah* (National Assembly) is the highest body of government, consisting of executive, legislative, and judicial representatives elected by the people, and at least 50 prominent leaders appointed by the president. Local government is carried on in provinces, districts, cities, and wards. The president is the chief of state and the prime minister is the chief of government. In 1992 rebel (*mujahideen*, or guerrilla) forces of various ethnic groups overthrew the government of Afghanistan. A temporary government with representation from various factions was formed. For administrative purposes, the country is divided into 31 provinces, though some people do not recognize the two most recently formed. The parliament and government offices are in the Dar ul-Aman Palace in Kabul.

Religion: Islam is the state's official religion. Almost 99 percent of the people are Muslim. 80 percent of the Muslims are Sunni and the rest are Shiite. There are small minority groups of Hindus, Sikhs, and Jews.

Ethnic Composition: Various ethnic groups and subgroups with different languages and dialects live in Afghanistan. The ethnic and tribal pride and affiliations are stronger than the national sentiment. Pushtuns live primarily in the southern and eastern parts where some are still nomads. Tajiks live in the Kabul and Badakhshan areas of the northeast and in the Herat region. Nuristanis live in the east, and Hazaras in the central highland region. Chahar Aimaks, Uzbeks, and Turkmens are Sunni Muslims of Turkic or Mongol origin living in the north and northwest.

Language: Pushtu (also called Psshto) and Dari (a form of Persian) are the national languages. Pushtuns speak Pushtu and the Tajiks speak Dari. The Nuristani people speak Kafiri dialects. Uzbek is spoken in northern Afghanistan. The Hazaras speak Dari and people of Turkic or Mongol origins speak Turkic dialects.

National Flag: Afghanistan's national flag was adopted by the Ruling Council in 1992. There are three equal horizontal stripes of black, white, and green. The inscription "God is Great" is centered on the black stripe, and another inscription, "There is no God but Allah, and Muhammad is the Prophet of Allah," is centered on the white stripe in the middle.

National Emblem: A rising sun surrounded by two sheaves of wheat bound together at the base and sides with ribbons in the national color.

National Anthem: *"Garam shah la garam shah"* ("Become hot, become hotter").

National Calendar: In addition to the Gregorian calendar, a solar and a lunar calendar are used. The Afghan year 1375 runs from March 1996 to March 1997.

Money: The Afghani (Af) is a paper currency of 100 puls. In early 1996, 4,750 Afghanis were equal to $1 US.

Membership in International Organizations: The Colombo Plan, United Nations (UN), and Economic Cooperation Organization (ECO).

Weights and Measures: The metric system has officially been adopted but traditional weights are still used.

Population: 1994 estimates 16,903,000 (excluding Afghan refugees outside the country); density is 67 persons per sq. mi. (26 persons per sq km). 81 percent live in rural areas and 19 percent live in cities. Nearly one-fifth of the people are nomadic.

Cities:
```
Kabul . . . . . . . . . . 700,000*
Qandahar  . . . . . . . . . . 225,500
Herat . . . . . . . . . . 177,300
Mazar-i Sharif . . . . . . . . . 130,600
```
(Population based on 1988 estimates, *1993)

GEOGRAPHY

Border: Pakistan is to the east and south. Turkmenistan, Uzbekistan, and Tajikistan are to the north. Iran is to the west, and China is to the northeast. Total length of international borders is 3,585 mi. (5,770 km).

Coastline: No direct access to the sea. Surrounded by land on all four sides.

Land: This landlocked mountainous country in south-central Asia is located at a strategic spot on the north-south and east-west trade routes. Three-fourths of the country's land area is mountainous. The average elevation in Afghanistan is about 4,000 ft. (1,200 m); some of the peaks in the Hindu Kush mountains rise above 21,000 ft. (6,400 m).

The Hindu Kush range separates the rich fertile northern provinces from the rest of the country and divides Afghanistan into the central highlands, the northern plains, and the southwestern plateau. The central highland region, with about 62 percent of the total area of the country, is mountainous with deep narrow valleys; this region is a continuation of the Himalayan mountain chain. The northern plain region, with 15 percent of the land, is agricultural, heavily populated, and contains rich mineral resources. The southern plateau, with 23 percent of the total land, is a region of high plateaus, sandy deserts, and semi-deserts; the Rigestan Desert spreads over about one-fourth of this section.

The Khyber Pass connects the cities of Kabul (Afghanistan) and Peshawar (Pakistan). The pass, governed by the Pakistan Khyber Agency, has a caravan track and a hard-surface road.

Highest Point: Mt. Nowshak, 24,557 ft. (7485 m).

Lowest Point: In Sistan Basin at 1,640 ft. (500 m) above sea level.

Rivers and Lakes. As Afghanistan has no seacoast, most of the water drains within the country. Amu Darya (ancient Oxus River) makes the northern boundary and separates Afghanistan from the central Asian highlands. The Kabul, Helmand, Harirud, and the Arghandab are other major rivers. The Helmand River provides water for several irrigation projects in the southwestern region. The Hamun-i Saberi is a major swampy lake. Five small lakes in the central highlands are known as Band-e Amir.

Plant Life: Forest area has been shrinking because of reckless cutting, and presently covers less than 5 percent of the country. Trees supply wood for construction, furniture, and fuel. Arctic and alpine flora thrive at high altitudes and arid-zone plants are common in the deserts. Pine, fir, and cedar trees grow as tall as 180 ft. (55 m) in the high mountains; oak, walnut, alder, ash, and juniper trees grow at lower altitudes. Rose, honeysuckle, hawthorn, currant, and gooseberry shrubs are common. Afghanistan is particularly rich in such medicinal plants as rue, wormwood, and asafetida.

Wildlife: Afghanistan's fauna include wild sheep, mountain goats, ibex, gazelles, wild dogs, and wild cats; wolves, foxes, hyenas, and jackals live in the mountains. Smaller animals include the mongoose, mole, shrew, hedgehog, bat, and several types of rats. Pheasants, quails, cranes, pelicans, snipes, partridges, and crows are common. About 100 species of wildfowl and other birds occur. Trout and salmon are common in the mountain streams.

Climate: The typical continental dry climate is marked by seasonal extremes. Very cold winters and hot summers are typical of the semi-arid highlands. The northeastern mountainous region has a subarctic climate with dry and bitter cold winters. The temperatures vary greatly from 120° F (48.8° C) in Jalalabad in July to –24° F (–31° C) at Kabul in the winter. Rainfall, averaging about 10 to 12 in. (25 to 30 cm), is concentrated between December and April, and decreases from east to west. In the arid regions of the southwest, precipitation of less than

5 in. (12.7 cm) is common. Most of the country experiences hot, dry, and cloudless weather in summer.

Greatest Distance: North-South, 630 mi. (1012 km).
                                    East-West, 820 mi. (1320 km).

Area: 251,773 sq. mi. (652 089 sq km).

ECONOMY AND INDUSTRY

Agriculture: Only half of the land available for agriculture is under actual cultivation, but that area provides livelihood for 85 percent of the population. Irrigation is of vital significance, and about one-third of the agricultural area is irrigated. Farms are small in size and farmers still use ancient tools and methods of agriculture, with little or no mechanization or fertilizers. Wheat is the principal crop; other crops are cotton, maize (corn), barley, fruits, pistachios, sugar beets, and sugarcane. The opium poppy is the most profitable, but illegal, crop grown extensively in Afghanistan. It is largely processed in Pakistan and exported to the United States, Europe, Iran, and India.

Livestock provide meat, dairy products, leather, skins, and wool. Sheep, lambs, cattle, donkeys, and goats are raised by seminomadic Afghans. The karakul sheep are world famous for their skins with glossy, curly wool. Camels, donkeys, and horses are used for transportation.

Mining: The country is rich in coal, natural gas, salt, uranium, chromium, iron ore, silver, gold, fluorite, talc, mica, copper, and semiprecious stones such as amethysts, rubies, and lapis lazuli. It is the world's leading producer of lapis lazuli, a dark blue stone mainly used in jewelry. First-quality emeralds are being mined once again. Some iron ore has been discovered, but it is located at high elevations and is difficult to mine. Hydroelectricity and thermal power supplies about three-fourths of the total energy used.

Manufacturing: Afghanistan ranks among the world's least developed countries in terms of industrial output. The uncertain political situation is one of the main reasons why industrial development has been slow. Manufacturing and industry are limited to cotton milling, cement, steel smelting, and copper smelting. Handicrafts such as carpets and rugs contribute more to the national economy than industry. Afghan woolen rugs are world famous for their style and color combination, with the best rugs being from Dalatabad and Herat. Often children are involved in the backbreaking job of rug-making. Other handicrafts include leather goods, gold and silver jewelry, woodworking, miniature paintings, glassware, silk, hand-loomed textiles, and pottery.

Transportation: Many rural areas are almost inaccessible to vehicles because of the damage to roads done by war. People walk, ride animals, or use horse-carts to visit other villages. There are only about 6 mi. (10 km) of railroads. In the late 1980s, there were 11,900 mi. (19 200 km) of roads, only half of which are paved. Buses, minibuses, and bicycles are the chief means of transportation in the cities, and very few people own automobiles. International airports are at Kabul and Qandahar.

Communication: 15 daily newspapers are published in Dari and Pushtu, and a few in English. The television and radio services are owned by the government. Radio service is more widely available than television. In the early 1990s, there was one radio receiver per 14 persons, one television set per 200 persons, and one telephone per 150 persons.

Trade: Chief imports are machinery, minerals, petroleum and petroleum products, sugar, motor vehicles, and textiles. Major import sources are Russia, Japan, Singapore, India, China, and South Korea. Chief export items are dried fruits and nuts, carpets, rugs, cotton, and karakul wool, skin, and hides. Major export destinations are Russia, Germany, and India.

EVERYDAY LIFE

Health: Medical facilities are scarce and limited, especially in rural areas. Only major cities have hospitals or clinics. In 1995 life expectancy at 42 years for males and 43 years for females was the lowest in Asia, and one of the lowest in the world. The infant-mortality rate at 161 per 1,000 live births is among the highest in the world. During the civil war, many children were killed or maimed by land mines and rockets. Malnutrition, malaria, measles, and tuberculosis are the major health problems. Unclean drinking water is the cause of many intestinal diseases. In the early 1990s, there were 6,500 persons per physician and 2,000 persons per hospital bed.

Education: Compulsory elementary education begins at age seven and lasts for eight years. Secondary education begins at age fifteen and lasts four years. There is a chronic shortage of school buildings and teachers as many buildings were destroyed and many teachers and scholars were killed during the civil war. Traditional education in rural areas was limited to Islamic teachings for boys by the local *mullah,* a religious leader; girls are even less likely to go to school than boys. Schoolbooks were altered during the 1980s to promote the Communist ideology; this policy has since been discarded.

Higher education consists of teacher training, vocational, and industrial colleges; there are universities at Kabul, Herat, Mazar-i Sharif, and Qandahar. In the late 1980s, there were 8 vocational colleges, 15 technical colleges, and 5 universities including an Islamic University at Kabul. Afghanistan has one of the highest illiteracy rates (over 70 percent) in Asia. In the early 1990s, the literacy rate was about 29 percent. The government is trying to encourage adult literacy by offering literacy courses.

Holidays:
>Nau-roz (New Year's Day, Iranian Calendar), March 21
>Liberation Day, April 18
>Revolution Day, April 27
>Worker's Day, May 1
>Independence Day, August 18

Holidays such as Ramadan, Id al-Fitr, Id al-Adha, Ashura, and Roze-Maulud are dependent on the Islamic lunar calendar and vary from year to year.

Culture: Written Afghan literature is very limited as the majority of the people cannot read or write; spoken poetry thus developed as the major literary form. Afghans pass on their tribal history by having a talented person recite the entire family relationship of the clan with stories of historic events. The Blue Mosque in Mazar-i Sharif is reputed to house the tomb of the Caliph Ali, son-in-law of Prophet Muhammad. A fifteenth-century mosque is in Herat.

Society: Islam permeates the daily life of the Afghans. Family ties are very strong, and birth, marriage, and death are times of social gatherings. A religious leader is an integral part of a village, dictating all aspects of life. Society is centered around the extended family, which may have three or four generations living under the same roof. A father or grandfather is generally the most important person in a family. Traditionally in the male-dominated Afghan society women were not given much freedom, but since 1965 when women received the right to vote, they have officially been given equal status with men and are increasingly taking part in public life; recently they have become television news commentators, bank workers, and most of all schoolteachers—some 75 percent of the teachers are women. Women do all cooking, washing, cleaning, taking care of children, and, in rural areas, they also do light farming. Women often spend their adult lives in *purdah* (seclusion) and are not seen by males who are not close family members.

Civil War/Refugees: In the fourteen years of war from 1979 to 1993, more than a million people died, more than 5 million fled the country and became refugees in Pakistan, and Iran, nearly 100,000 acres (40,469 hectares) of forest-land was destroyed, and an estimated 500,000 farm animals were killed. Soon after the Soviet invasion in 1979, it is estimated that about 3.2 million Afghan refugees fled to Pakistan and 2.1 million to Iran to escape civil war at home. The civil war extensively damaged roads and bridges, making movement of people even more difficult.

Dress: Western clothing has been largely adopted by Afghan men in the urban areas, but return to more traditional clothing is encouraged by the mujahideen. Traditionally, both men and women wear long cotton shirts and baggy trousers. Men often wear turbans and a dress coat or vest over the long shirt. Women may wear a shawl, and a long bright skirt over trousers. Women often wear a *chaderi*, a long covering that reveals only the women's eyes. Almost everyone wears heavy sheepskin or quilted coats and flat woolen caps to keep out the bitter cold of winter.

Housing: Seminomadic Afghans live in tents that are easy to take apart and carry. A typical rural house is made of sun-dried mud-bricks and has several rooms. Several of such mud houses are surrounded by high mud walls that have multipurpose use, such as providing privacy for women and security from enemies. Homes generally have a special room where male friends are received by the male host. A small percentage of the urban population lives in modern apartment buildings.

Food: *Pilaf,* a dish of rice cooked with meat and vegetables, is the national dish. *Kebabs* are chunks of meat placed on a skewer, usually with vegetables, and grilled over fire. Whole wheat bread called *nan* is either baked or fried, and served with almost every meal to be used as an eating utensil. Major food items are tomatoes, spinach, potatoes, peas, carrots, cucumbers, and eggplants. A very sweet desert is *jelabi*. Fruits, such as apples, pears, peaches, apricots, grapes, plums, cherries, pomegranates, and melons, are plentiful in the Afghan diet. Black or green *chai* (tea) is served with almost every meal. Nomads precook their rice before long journeys to cut down on cooking time. People strictly follow the Islamic prohibition against alcohol and pork.

Sports and Recreation: Wrestling and weight lifting are traditionally the two most popular sports in Afghanistan. Other favorite games are soccer, volleyball, field hockey, and golf. The traditional game of *buzkashi* requires skill and horsemanship as riders try to carry the headless carcass of a calf or goat over a goal. Most leisure activities are centered around the family and relatives. The traditional musical instruments are drums, a stringed gourd (similar to a lute), and a clarinet-like instrument called a *surnai*. War dances, such as the *attan,* are performed by men where they dance around a stake or fire and swing swords or guns in their right hands. During Ramadan (a month of dawn-to-dusk fasting), families and friends gather in the evening to break the fast and socialize.

Social Welfare: Social welfare is considered a function of religion and charitable programs. The Afghan society is relatively free from social problems such as unemployment, alcoholism, and juvenile delinquency. People in general take care of their old family members and needy relatives. The Red Crescent Society (Islamic), the equivalent of the Red Cross, cares for medically needy people.

IMPORTANT DATES

522 B.C.—Zarathustra, the founder of the Zoroastrian (Parsee) religion, is killed in the region of present-day Afghanistan.

328 B.C.—Alexander the Great enters what is now Afghanistan, and crosses the Helmand River to capture Bactria.

A.D. 642—Arab invasion of Afghanistan; Islam is introduced.

1219—Mongol invasion under Genghis Khan; many cities are destroyed.

1370–1505—Golden period of peace and prosperity in Afghan history.

1507—The Timurids are conquered by Muhammad Shaybani Khan.

1719—Herat rebels against Persia's (present-day Iran) Shiite persecution and declares independence.

1747—A confederation of Durrani tribes elects Ahmad Shah Abdali "king,"and he founds the royal dynasty that rules Afghanistan until 1973; Qandahar becomes the first capital of the unified Afghanistan

1776—The capital is moved from Qandahar to Kabul.

1836—Dost Muhammad declares an Islamic holy war on Sikh leader Ranjit Singh of Punjab.

1838—British troops invade Afghanistan and advance to Qandahar.

1839–42—The First Anglo-Afghan War.

1852—Mazar-i Sharif is included in Afghan territory.

1878–80—The Second Anglo-Afghan War.

1893—The Durand Agreement establishes Afghanistan as a buffer state between the Russian and the British Indian frontiers.

1904—Country's first secondary school is opened.

1907—Habibullah visits British India.

1918—*Light of Children,* a children's journal, is published.

1919—The Third Anglo-Afghan War; Afghanistan becomes independent; Habibullah assassinated, and Amanullah takes the throne.

1923—First constitution is adopted.

1928—Bacha Saqqao, a Tajik hero, takes power and proclaims himself Habibullah Ghazi II.

1929—Amanullah abdicates the throne and flees to India; Nadir Shah takes the throne.

1931—A new constitution is proclaimed.

1932—First bank is founded; the University of Kabul is established.

1933—Mohammad Nadir Shah is assassinated; Zahir Shah becomes king.

1944–45—Internal revolt against the ruling king.

1946—Afghanistan is admitted to the United Nations.

1952—Elections are held for the National Parliament.

1956—An earthquake kills about 2,000 people.

1961—Afghanistan cuts off diplomatic relations with Pakistan.

1964—A new constitution providing a National Parliament with two houses, a House of the People and a House of the Elders, is approved.

1965—Afghan women vote for the first time in the national elections.

1972—People are faced with widespread grain shortage; famine kills thousands.

1973—Monarchy comes to an end with Mohammad Daoud seizing power; 1964 constitution is abolished; Afghanistan is declared a republic.

1975—Daoud renews a Soviet-Afghan Treaty of Neutrality and Non-Aggression for ten years.

1977—A new constitution provides for only one political party.

1978—The Great *Saur* (April) coup abolishes the 1977 constitution and establishes the Democratic Republic of Afghanistan under the People's Democratic Party of Afghanistan (PDPA); a 20-year Treaty of Friendship and Good Neighborliness is signed between Afghanistan and the Soviet Union; the Tillya-Tepe archeological site is excavated.

1979—Government's five-year economic plan is published; US ambassador Adolph Dubs is kidnapped and killed; the United States cuts its aid to Afghanistan; Soviet Union sends 80,000 troops to invade Afghanistan and overthrows Hafizullah Amin; pro-Moscow hard-liner Babrak Karmal becomes president.

1980—Afghanistan is suspended from the Conference of Islamic States.

1979–89—Over 14,000 Soviet soldiers die in the ten-year Soviet occupation of Afghanistan.

1981—Negotiations begin under United Nations auspices for withdrawal of the Soviet forces from Afghanistan.

1984—Mujahideen receive outside support from countries such as the United States and China, against the pro-Soviet national government.

1985—A meeting of the National Assembly is called, followed by a meeting of the tribes; Islamic Union of Afghan Mujahideen (IUAM) is formed; a new constitution is ratified.

1986—Former head of the secret police, Dr. Mohammad Najibullah, is appointed head of the government.

1987—Najibullah is unanimously elected president in a session of *Loya Jirgah;* a new constitution is ratified; the country's name is changed to the Republic of Afghanistan; the Islamic Coalition Council of Afghanistan (ICAA) is formed by an eight-group alliance of Shiite parties supported by Iran.

1988—IUAM announces a 28-member interim coalition government for an Islamic State of Afghanistan; Soviet Union begins withdrawal of troops.

1989—All Soviet troops (numbering about 115,000) are withdrawn from Afghanistan; a state of emergency is declared by Najibullah.

1990—An unsuccessful coup attempted to overthrow Najibullah.

1991—Rebel leaders reject a truce proposed by Najibullah.

1992—Najibullah is forced out of government and the mujahideen take over Kabul under Commander Ahmed Shah Masoud; amnesty is given to all members of the former government except Najibullah, who remains under UN protection in Kabul; sale of alcohol is banned; women are required to cover their heads and wear Islamic dress; the National Assembly is dissolved and the Communist Party is outlawed; UN announces $10 million in aid for food and medicine.

1993—Some 120,000 Tajik refugees flee across the border from Tajikistan into Afghanistan; Burhanuddin Rabbani is elected president in an election with only one candidate.

1994—Gulbuddian Hekmatyar unites with General Abdul Rashid Dostam to launch an attack to oust Rabbani; his militia launches an air attack on Kabul; government forces finally capture 1,000 members of the Dostam loyalists; between January and June, some 2,500 Afghans are killed in rebel struggles; Supreme Court extends Rabbani's presidential term in June for six more months;

1995—The UN tries to negotiate the transfer of power from President Rabbani to a broad-based council; Rabbani refuses to yield powers.

1996—The UN says Kabul contains more land mines than any other city in the world; there is little left of the city.

IMPORTANT PEOPLE

Abdur Rahman Khan (1830?–1901), amir of Kabul and founder of modern Afghanistan; reigned from 1880 to 1901 and established a strong centralized government.

Ahmad Shah Abdali (1724–1772), a Muslim emperor and a national hero; he is considered the founder of the state of Afghanistan; he changed his dynastic name from Abdali to Durrani.

Timur Shah Abdali (–1793), a son of Ahmad Shah Abdali; his reign is marked by putting down rebellions.

Amanullah Khan (1892–1960), third son of Habibullah Khan; seized power in 1919 and initiated the Third Anglo-Afghan War; changed his title from *amir* to *padshah* (king); introduced the first constitution and secular codes of laws; advocated the removal of veil for women and founded coeducational schools; abdicated the throne in 1929 and fled to India and then to Europe where he died without regaining power.

Hafizullah Amin (1929–1979), Khalq political party leader; took over from Nur Mohammad Taraki in 1979 and became president of the Revolutionary Council.

Abdullah Ansari (1005-88), poet and saint of Herat.

Ustad Kamaluddin Bihzad, court painter during Timurid period.

al-Biruni (973–1048), a scientist, historian, and encyclopedist at the time of Mahmud of Ghazni.

Mohammad Daoud (1909-78), prime minister from 1953 to 1963; promoted modernization, economic improvement, and educational reforms; overthrew the last Afghan king and declared Afghanistan a republic in 1973; ruled as a dictator and was killed with his family in a military coup.

Dost Muhammad Khan (1789–1862), leader and founder of the powerful Barakzai dynasty; assumed the title of *amir* (chief) and unified the country.

Firdausi (935–1020), Persian poet; wrote one of the world's great epics, *Shahnameh* (Book of Kings).

Habibullah Khan (1872 –1919), son of Abdur Rahman; ruled Afghanistan from 1901 to 1919; like his father, he encouraged modern technology and strong centralized government.

Gulbuddin Hekmatyar, a Pushtun mujahideen leader.

Jami (1414-1492), Persian poet.

Babrak Karmal (1929–), leader of the Parcham party; installed as a new leader by Soviet Union after Soviet invasion in 1979; he tried to modify the land and social reform programs; chief of state from 1979 to 1986.

Abdul Aziz Londoni, a merchant who dealt with tea, spices, cotton, and karakul skins in the 1920s; he helped establish an economic base for the development of the country.

Mahmud of Ghazni (998–1030), Turkish emperor; consolidated the conquests of his predecessors and turned Ghazni into a great cultural center.

Mir Wais Khan, a leader of the Hotaki Ghilzai tribe who led a successful revolt against the Safavid Persian governor in 1719; briefly conquered Persia.

Commander Ahmed Shah Masoud, the military commander under Rabbani, responsible for defending the government against attacks by troops of Gulbuddin Hekmatyar.

Nadir Shah (1688-1747), the Persian king who conquered Afghanistan in 1737.

(Mohammad) Nadir Shah (1880–1933), a cousin of Amanullah; took power from Habibullah Ghazi II; began a program of reform.

Dr. Mohammad Najibullah (1947–), former head of the Afghan secret police; he was installed as head of the pro-Soviet government in 1986 but was forced out in 1992; rebels want to try him for war crimes; under the protection of the UN mission at Kabul in 1996.

Qavam-ud-Din, architect during the heyday of Herat.

Burhanuddin Rabbani (1942–), a mujahideen leader of the *Jamiat-I-Islami,* "Society of Islam Party;" president in the early 1990s.

Sher Ali Khan (1825 –1879), third son of Dost Muhammad; amir, 1868-78.

Nur Mohammad Taraki (1917–1979), president of the revolutionary council and prime minister in 1978-79; founded PDPA.

Mahmud Beg Tarzi, an Afghan nationalist; published periodicals such as *Torch of the News* and *Light of Children;* his daughter, Soraya, married Amanullah.

Zahir Shah (1914–); son of Mohammed Nadir Shah; took the title of king of Afghanistan in 1933; was deposed by a coup in 1973.

Compiled by Chandrika Kaul, Ph.D.

INDEX

Page numbers that appear in boldface type indicate illustrations.

About the Author

Dr. Leila Merrell Foster is a lawyer, United Methodist minister, and clinical psychologist with degrees from Northwestern University and Garrett Evangelical Theological Seminary. She is author of books and articles on a variety of subjects. Dr. Foster has traveled extensively and is particularly interested in archeology. Other countries she has written about in the Enchantment of the World series include Bhutan, Iraq, Lebanon, Jordan, and Saudi Arabia.